MY THREE YEARS
IN THE
MARINE CORPS

D1562421

MY THREE YEARS
IN THE
MARINE CORPS

By

RAY MERRELL
Marine Raider

Edited by Helen Merrell

To James Chambers + Rose
My ole pal
Ray Merrell
"Gung-Ho!"

This story is an account of my experiences in the United States Marine Corps and the Marine Raiders during WWII.

It is compiled from my diary entries, memories and letters written to Helen in tents, mess halls, galleys, foxholes and behind trees, by candlelight, flashlight and lantern.

Revised second edition.
Copyright © 2003 by Ray Merrell.
Printed in the United States.
All rights reserved.

ISBN: 1-58597-238-X

Library of Congress Control Number: 2003114733

A division of Squire Publishers, Inc.
4500 College Blvd.
Leawood, KS 66211
1/888/888-7696
www.leatherspublishing.com

Dedication

Dedicated to

my daughter, Deborah Sue Hopper,

and

my son, Robert Alan Merrell.

TABLE OF CONTENTS

Joining the Marines, 11-17-42

I WAS 19 YEARS OLD, working at the shoe factory in Marshall, Missouri, Tuesday, November 17, 1942. I was paid by piece work, and we had work orders that told us what to make up. My work was on the first part of the shoe, getting the shoe last ready for the uppers. We had to do so many racks each day. We were making military shoes for the Army and Marines. One morning the supervisors were riding us to get more work done, so three of us (Sammy Hayslip, Shorty Pace and I) walked out about 10 a.m. and went to Sedalia to join the Marines. We had decided we would rather wear the shoes than make them.

I knew my dad would not be pleased, as he had wanted me to join the Navy. His reasoning was that the Navy always would have a bed and good food. I had not told him I was going to join the Marines, but when I got home from Sedalia, my draft papers were there in the morning mail.

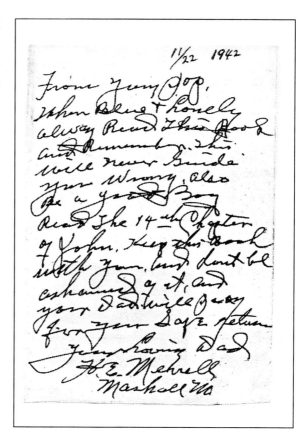

That softened him up a bit, and he gave me a Bible with this inscription written in it when I left for the Marines.

The Sunday after I joined the Marines, my mom and pop had a family dinner for me. All my fam-

1

Helen and Ray

ily was there — Ernie and Frank; Norma and Pete of Kansas City; Paul, Dorothy and Jimmy; Mildred and Raymond; Nelson, Dorothy and Cora Lea (Lee) of Marshall, and my girlfriend, Helen Treece of Herndon.

Helen and I had been dating since May 3rd. We had a wonderful summer going to

Helen

parties, movies, roller skating, carnivals, the fair, dances, taking a sightseeing ride in an airplane, and in the fall going to football games. We enjoyed just being with our friends, and I liked going to Helen's folks. I enjoyed them, also the green grass, trees, flowers and the quiet of the country. I thought

a lot about my family and all those things over the three years I was gone. Before I left, I made a date with Helen for "tomorrow night" when I get home.

I had a dark green Hudson Essex Terraplane car with light pea-green fenders. It didn't always run, but I would find other ways to get out to Helen's on the farm, either by double-dating or by using my dad's car.

Terraplane needs a drink at Bucksnort School.

Ray Merrell
St. Louis, Mo.
November 26, 1942

I gave Helen a gold expansion bracelet and matching heart-shaped locket for Christmas before I left for the Marines.

Sammy, Shorty and I went back to Sedalia November 25th and took a train to St. Louis, arriving there at 1 p.m. We took our physicals that afternoon. I was the only one to pass, and after Sammy and Shorty left to go back home, I felt pretty lost and lonesome. We were at the Reed Hotel, so to have something to do, I went to an Andrews Sisters movie that night. The next day our fingerprints were taken, and they assigned us a Marine uniform (one size fits all) and took our picture. I hadn't gotten acquainted with anyone, so didn't have anyone to fool around with. It already seemed like I had been gone for months.

On the Train, St. Louis to San Diego, 11-27-42 to 11-30-42

WE LEFT ST. LOUIS on the train Friday, November 27, about 6 p.m. On the train I met Robert (Red) Lindsay, who was from St. Louis. He was a little older than I, and he called me "Junior." We rode the train all night, going through Omaha, then North Platte, Nebraska, about noon the next day. We were in North Platte about 10 minutes, but the ladies of the area welcomed us and served us all kinds of sandwiches, cookies and pop. It was a welcome break.

You can read all about the ladies

Robert (Red) Lindsay

who met all the trains going through North Platte during WW II in Bob Green's book, "Once Upon a Town." You'll like it!

We were on the train all night again; I rode in the upper deck. I had tried the lower deck, but didn't sleep well there. We traveled through Cheyenne, Wyoming, Saturday evening and on to Salt Lake City at 1 p.m. Sunday, arriving in Los Angeles at 11 a.m. Monday, then on to San Diego. From the train in San Diego we went by bus to the Marine Corps Recruit Depot, arriving there about 5 p.m. I had sent Helen a card every day, and Red wrote to his wife and daughter every day.

Boot Camp, 12-1-42 to 1-20-43

WHEN WE GOT to the boot camp at 5 p.m., the drill instructor, Corporal J.W. Montgomery, was already mad that his leave had been cancelled because of new troops coming in, so we were already in trouble without having done anything. He certainly let us know who was boss. We were in the 1127th Platoon and were issued an M-1 rifle. When the recruits who had been there one day looked at Red with his bushy red hair and me with my black curly hair, they told us we would be sorry when we got our haircuts. We knew what they meant the next day when we were given our crew cuts; there was no mercy. We were issued our uniforms that day.

We drilled every day; the drill instructor would tell us "the other left" if we messed up. If you messed up often, you got to drill

After the crew cut

by yourself. We ran the obstacle course, had training and learned about rifles. I was in good shape and always ran the obstacle course more than was required.

There were 30 of us staying in tents for three or four weeks. We had to disassemble all cigarette butts while there. Then we moved into cabins (sort of). When the drill instructor said to fall out (for roll call), I guess we didn't get out fast enough, as he said, "When I say I want you out, I want you out." The second time we fell out, he said, "Get back in there, and get out here when I tell you." The third time we fell out, we were climbing all over each other and just about broke down the door getting out.

Two weeks after we started boot camp, Tyrone Power, the movie star, reported in to base for active duty. We were warned not to follow him around or ask for his autograph. We didn't see much of him.

On one rifle inspection, the strap on my rifle wasn't tight enough (couldn't play a tune on it), so I had to do 100 push-ups with my rifle, lifting it over my head. The rifle got so heavy it brought me up on my tiptoes. Then the drill instructor said, "Rest and hold it out in front," and that brought me on my toes also. I thought my punishment would never end!

We had good food to eat at camp, all we could eat of pork chops, ice cream and all.

During the eight weeks we were in boot camp, we went to the rifle range at Camp Matthews for three to five days. At the camp we scoured our mess gear with sand to get the aluminum coating off before we could eat. I qualified for sharpshooter while at Camp Matthews. *(I have donated my rifle scoring book to the San Diego Marine Raider Museum.)*

During boot camp I was one of seven chosen to attend an Honor Dance. Those chosen were the most popular with the others and had qualified as

---

SELECTED FOR HONOR DANCE
Pvt. R.L. Merrell is liked in
Platoon 1127, Marine Corps

Pvt. R.L. Merrell has made a hit with the other members of Platoon 1127, U.S. Marines, San Diego, for Pvt. Robert Lindsay writes to the Democrat-News that Private Merrell was the first man of seven chosen by the platoon corporal to attend an honor dance in San Diego. Selection of the seven was on the basis of the members who were most popular with the other fellows in the platoon, but only those could be chosen who had qualified as sharpshooter, which is the next highest honor of a rifleman in the Marine Corps.

Private Lindsay writes that "We are proud to have such a man as Private Merrell in 1127." Incidentally, he states that Private Merrell showed himself to be a good dancer and a good talker at the dance.

sharpshooter. When we got back from the dance, my "buddies" had short-sheeted my bed. Red Lindsay made a big deal out of the dance, and got a big laugh out of sending this article to the *Marshall Democrat News.*

I wasn't the first one chosen, and I wasn't the most popular, but I **had** qualified as sharpshooter.

While we were at the rifle range, some of the guys were sitting around talking about what they didn't like about the Marine Corps.

People are amazed when I tell them that I was a Marine. For some reason, I don't look like one — and I certainly don't act like one. But I was, and — according to God, or the tradition of the Corps — I will always be a Marine.

In every Marine's life, there is one man he remembers as long as he lives — and that is his Drill Instructor. The D.I. has to take raw recruits and turn them into fighting machines. He does this through threats, psychological terror, physical exercises and hazing — when no one is looking. The whole process is built around fear.

The brainwashing never stops, morning, noon and night. No matter what you do right, you are told that you are doing it wrong. The D.I.s rip up your bed after you worked on it for an hour. Your shoes are never shined enough, your footlocker is judged to be a mess, and your replies to questions are never satisfactory. You are constantly told what a hopeless, miserable dingbat you are. Only the person who bore you could love you. The purpose of all this is to break you down and then rebuild you into the person the Marine Corps wants — one who will never question an order, who will always worry about his buddy and who, someday, will walk as tall as John Wayne.

My drill instructor was Cpl. Peter Martin Bonardi of Elmhurst, N.Y. Every Marine who goes through boot camp maintains in later life that his D.I. was the toughest, meanest man in the whole U.S. Marine Corps. It was no contest — mine was. Don't listen to other Marines. Trust me.

Bonardi never ran out of tortures. He made me clean the barracks head with a toothbrush. Then he forced me to march around with rocks in my pack, because I was brushing my teeth when he called everyone out for muster.

It doesn't take long before your D.I. becomes the most important person in your life. I was more afraid of him than any other thing. For example, when I saw the Parris Island obstacle course for the first time, I froze.

Bonardi told us that we had the choice of doing it or going to sick bay and having his boot removed from the seat of our pants. It was his way of motivating us. I completed the course — not once, but twice. Bonardi never even said "Thank you."

I was finishing up my tour. All of us had hardened. There is nothing like a 20-mile hike with a full pack and one canteen of water to convince you that you can not only lick the enemy, but the U.S. Army and Navy, too.

On graduation day, Platoon 911 marched together for the last time on the parade grounds. In eight weeks, the D.I.s had accomplished their mission impossible. We may not have been seasoned Marines, but we looked like seasoned Marines. For the first time, Bonardi smiled before he said goodbye. We knew he was pleased, because he had won money on us from the Drill Instructor training the platoon in the next barracks.

By Art Buchwald
Published in the Kansas City Star

The corporal who was in charge was listening, and it was making him angry, so he took it out on us to let us know who was boss — again. After we went to bed and most of us were asleep, our drill instructor had us all fall out; however, we were dressed. When that was over, we got back in bed. When we were asleep again, he called for us to fall out a second time, then back to bed. Our drill instructor was Corporal Montgomery, who was still mad at us for getting his leave cancelled when we checked in to camp. He had us fall out yet a third time. This time he took a flashlight and checked to see if we had clean underwear and told us that would teach us to talk about what we didn't like about the Marines.

December 24th, on Red Cross stationery I wrote:

Dearest sweetheart,

I have only been gone one month, but it seems so long. It really rained while we were laying on the ground, and it was cold. We were in it all day target practicing. My cold is better, but don't know how it will be in the morning after laying on the wet, muddy ground all day.

We all put in some money, and the Corporal is going to get us some candy. We have to keep it secret so he won't get in trouble; he is nice sometimes. One of the corporals has a little radio we listen to some, but we can't gather around his bunk. We can hear a little music anyway.

When we were through with boot camp, the drill instructors softened up. They told us we would soon outrank them, and that they had to be hard on us to get us in shape.

Camp Elliott and Green's Farm, 1-20-43 to 3-11-43

January 20

Dearest sweetheart Helen,

We went to Camp Elliott for training, hiking in the hills and small mountains, getting in top physical shape. We went on an all-day hike, and one Marine got lost. We searched for him in the mountains and went out in the hills at night to fire tracer bullets so he could find his way back, but he never returned. He probably went AWOL.

7

I read your letters 'til I know them by heart, and I look at your pictures every night and every chance I get. I keep all your letters and read them over and over.

I sent Helen a blue handkerchief and scarf with the Marine emblem on it for her birthday.

February 7

Dearest Helen,

I went to the show this afternoon. It was Red Skelton in "Whistling in Dixie." After the show Red and I went to the PX and got a coke and a pint of strawberry ice cream. I also bought a hunting knife.

I just think of you as being on the other side of the mountains, with the mountains the only thing separating us.

February 11

Dearest Helen,

We had rifle inspection last night about 5:30; it took 1-1/2 hours. I got really tired standing at attention.

I received about 10 Marshall papers that had been held up. I read all the news and saw pictures of the boys who left for the Army. I knew most of them. Must not be anyone around but school boys, but I guess you can take your pick out of those, can't you?

Helen is a dark-haired, brown-eyed sophomore in Marshall High School, riding the big yellow bus from the farm, and playing basketball on the Marshall High School girls team (wearing the ugly green baggy gym suits, she says). Her good friends are Vesta Thomas and Eleanor Scott. Helen's middle name is Elizabeth, and when I tease her I call her "Lizzie." Some of her friends call her "Teddy."

In Helen's junior year in high school a neighbor, friend and classmate, Gene Thomas (17 years old), drove the bus for Marshall High School. He drove an old one-seated Chevrolet car that had been made into a pickup. He would come by her house and pick her up; then they would go to Herndon to get the bus which was stored in a shed there. After school he would drive the bus back to Herndon and then on home in the pickup, dropping Helen off on the way. In those years a high school student was trusted to be a school bus driver.

We learned to fire the Thompson Machine Gun. It shoots really fast. For a dime we got in to see the movies in San Diego, and we also went skating. I liked the songs, "When the Lights Go On Again, " "For Me and My Gal" and "Moonlight Becomes You." I got very homesick, and I got the feeling that I would never get back. I don't get liberty this weekend because it is liberty from A to K. I guess I will go to the show here on the base and answer some letters I got from the boys at the factory.

February 14th we hiked out to Green's Farm; it was very hot. Six of the boys passed out, 28 were late. The late ones were put on mess duty. We were carrying heavy packs — two packs weighed 40 or 45 pounds, the rifle 10 pounds and the helmet 8 pounds. There was not a dry thread on any of us. I believe those steel helmets would finally make anyone bald-headed.

Green's Farm was a pretty place in a valley between all the small mountains. It used to be a farm ranch until the government took it over. We lived in tents, three to a tent. We had a little kerosene stove to heat water to shave and wash our face and hands. We had a PX about the size of a peanut box where we could get Cokes and Grapette. We took baths in a stream or in a bucket if the stream was too cold. The moon was shining bright at Green's Farm, and the crickets were chirping.

February 22

Dearest school kid,

We didn't go to school today; it has been raining hard. We have our packs, rifles and everything it takes to go into battle laying on our bunks ready to be inspected, and to get what we are supposed to have. We had clothing inspection to get more clothes.

They had on the bulletin board that we have this week of hikes, then we go to Camp Pendleton, 100 miles up the coast and 40 miles from Los Angeles, up in the mountains, of course. More mountains to hike over. I don't think it will be long before we go across. I will send you my watch if you won't think it is your fault if it quits running. If you get where you don't love me, you can give it to Dorothy or someone. I hope you will always love me, because I do you.

I live on 3rd Street, Hut 30; come up and see me sometime.

I saw in the Marshall paper where Marshall beat Slater. I guess you all are good. I also saw where you got a typing pin.

When we were dating, Helen was in a play one night at Hazel Grove Church. I showed up in my 1933 Essex Terraplane to see the play. When the play was over, I went out to my car and I had a flat tire. I had to jack up the car and put on a spare. The next day I went to a filling station to get the tire fixed, and there was no puncture. I really think one or some of Helen's old boyfriends let the air out of my tire. They were probably hiding behind a tombstone in the church cemetery laughing at me while I was changing the tire. It was a lot of work for a prank.

February 23

Hello, honey,

I received four letters; that makes up for out at Green's Farm. I didn't think you had forgotten me already. I got a letter from your old boyfriend. He said he sees you in the halls, but you don't have much to say.

Was the box of candy OK? I love to send you things to remind you of me. I hope I get back to see you. I know I will. I will be back, I hope and pray. I love you so much.

I got a letter from G.W. from out at Green's Farm. He is going home March 4th for nine days, the lucky boy. I wish I could. I would even go to school with you, just to be with you. On the radio they are singing "The East Bound Train Was Loaded." I wish I was on it.

We have Navy corpsmen who will go across with us, and they go on the hikes, too. They dress in Marine uniforms, and they are nice. Every time out at Green's Farm we had to wear the steel helmets. I got used to it at last.

February 24

Dearest Helen of mine,

We went on a hike today and didn't even take our packs. We didn't think we would go on a hike. We went about five miles north of Camp Elliott and crawled around in the brush in the big hills. At 11:30 we stopped under some trees and thought we would get to eat, but we didn't. They wanted to show us what we would have to do when we went across. We got really hungry, but couldn't do a thing about it. Boy, did I eat tonight!

February 25

Hi, Sugar,

They haven't found the fellow that got lost. They have lots of mail for him, and he isn't here to get it, so he must still be lost.

Some of the officers thought maybe he went over the hill and went home, but he still gets mail. I don't think he could live very long in those hills. When it is hot here, the big snakes are out running around, and I am scared of them. They strike at you and are poisonous, too. I don't feel so good tonight. We went on another hike today and didn't eat any dinner, but I will feel good in the morning.

February 28

Dearest sweetheart,

I won't get to write this week. We are going out in the mountains and live a whole week, sleep on the ground and eat field rations. I won't be able to get your letters, but you can keep writing if you want to. I will get them sometime.

We had sniper's school on Green's Farm. We went on all-day and all-night hikes, carrying our 25-pound hiking packs, our rifles and steel helmets. We lived out of our packs. They had given us two potatoes, one onion, some rice and prunes. One day five of us got hungry, so we hiked about a mile to a farmer's house and bought a hen. We boiled it, pin feathers and all, in an ammo can. The chicken and broth were really good.

There were 156 of us on one 29-mile hike. The lieutenants shot rifles to play like we were under enemy fire. When they started shooting, we would hit the "deck." The bullets would go just over our heads. One of the boys asked if they were shooting close, and about that time a bullet hit about a foot in front of him.

We went up one mountain that was two miles upgrade and others that were very steep. By the time we got there, 50 were in the first bunch and the rest came straggling in for two hours. I was eighth in the first bunch. I was really tired halfway up, but I just kept on; I guess it was the spirit that moved me, and I tried to keep up with the rest.

In the California mountains there was a good clear stream coming out of the mountains, so we lay down on our stomachs and drank out of the cold stream. We were hot and it tasted good.

The sergeants spotted a deer in the woods and killed it. I was close, and they used my knife to skin it and cut it up. We carried it back to camp. They divided it up, and we all got to cook some of it.

On one of our hikes another boy and I went over two or three hills to a farm house to ask for some water. The people were very nice and gave us water. They also fixed us two sandwiches and gave each of us a glass of milk.

During our training we were crawling down a mountain while the corporals and sergeants were shooting over our heads, when all of a sudden a guy started screaming. There was a rattlesnake in a culvert, coiled and ready to spring. The corporals and sergeants fired right in front of the guy's nose and killed the snake before it could strike.

Another time when we were ambushing each other and hiding in the bushes, one guy went to sleep, so we hung a dead rattlesnake on some sagebrush in front of him, then threw dirt clods at him to wake him. He didn't think it was too funny, but we did.

February 28

Hi, Sugar,

Friday night I was so homesick for you I couldn't get you off my mind. I couldn't even write I was so lonesome. Sometimes I wonder if I had better stop writing to you and let you forget me, but I love you too much. I get to feeling that I will never get back and it really makes me feel bad, because I want to see you so much. I wish I would get to come home before I go across, but there isn't much chance of that happening. I will be back sometime, I know. At least I have your picture, and I will have it with me at all times.

In our field rations we get six cans for a week. It is 2.50 oz. biscuit, 1.0 oz. confection, .50 oz. sugar, 25 oz. soluble coffee, and we get one pint of water over two days. We don't change clothes, only our sox. We don't shave. We cook one raw meal out there; each one cooks his own. We go out and try to hide so the sergeants and corporals can't find us for a week. We will build a little camp and try to keep out of the enemy's sight. I will write as soon as I get back. I will be thinking of you. Please don't forget me. That is the only thing I worry about. Be sure to write so I will get a letter at the end of this week.

March 2

Dearest Helen,

We went on a hike yesterday, but were called back last night. We are going to scout and sniper school for five weeks. I think we are waiting for the notice of what to do. We just got in from marching for our morning exercise. We hiked about 20 miles yesterday, with just one pack though.

Helen, I haven't gotten a letter from you for a few days, and it seems like a year. We didn't go to Camp Pendleton. They seem not to know where to send us. Bye — we are going somewhere.

March 5

Dearest Helen,

Well, here I am again, and glad to be back from the hills and living on canned rationing. I received five letters; it made me feel good. I really had to end that last letter fast.

It was about 10 a.m. one day when they said "fall out," so we did. They told us to get our packs ready ASAP. We got our packs and started out without lunch. We hiked about 12 miles. We had a canteen of water, one quart or less. When we got there, we were issued four small cans of rations. We had two cans of biscuits (round and hard like dog biscuits), one can of pork and beans, a piece of bacon, a small piece of steak, two onions, three potatoes and an orange. We had to eat Wednesday, Thursday and breakfast Friday. We slept on the ground and it started raining at 6 a.m. Thursday and didn't stop. We had to cook out in the rain. We camped on the side of a big hill. There were 21 of us in a bunch, and we set up a small camp with our shelter halves and ponchos. It turned water a little, but mostly strained it.

Thursday night we got hungry, so three of us went to a farmer's house about a mile away and bought two chickens and a dozen eggs. He gave us some salt. I dressed one of the chickens, dry-picked it, then singed and scalded it. I had some funny-looking pieces. We cooked it in an old can that we had scalded out good. We boiled it and made some good broth and drank it. It was a good meal and tasted great. We had fun even if we did get hungry.

After Green's Farm we went back to Camp Elliott. I went to the PX and weighed. I had lost nine pounds. We trained some more, hiking and crawling around in the brush in the mountains, until time to leave the U.S.A.

I have been here about three months and what a life! I have had a lot of good experiences and learned a lot. I really like it, even if I do get mad once in a while at things we have to do. It seems like I have been away from you, honey, for a long, long time. I hope I am never away from you again.

I just got out of the show, "Just Off Broadway," with Lloyd

Noland. It was a good show.

Monday afternoon they told us not to leave the squad room, that we would only have a moment's notice. We had roll call every two hours; we didn't get to go any place. All day Tuesday we had to do the same until 6 p.m. Then they gave us base liberty and told us to be in by 9 p .m. We thought we were going to be shipped out, but they have let us out now. I say we have three more weeks here — I don't know. We go on hikes the rest of this week and next and eat field rations. It rained today and we got soaked. Our rifles got wet, and they were hard to clean.

March 6

Dearest Sweetheart,

We had personal, barracks and rifle inspection; then we were off for the day. However, we could not leave the barracks for some reason. Yesterday we got our gas masks and shots in the arm.

I went to a U.S.O. show last night (Linda Darnell). It was good. Today I'm going to wash clothes, go swimming and go to a movie tonight.

Helen wrote that they had played a basketball game with Blackburn. She was going home, shampoo her hair, do her algebra, read a book, listen to the hit parade and write to me. She sometimes stays in town with Vesta, but usually rides the bus home.

On March 9th, I wrote a card that I was moving and would send a new address ASAP and that a card would be sent by the government when I got across.

We had packed our sea bags the night before, and they went out on a truck the next morning. They told us we would see them in a month or two, that we would have to live out of our packs until we got our sea bags. I had sent my medals and some things home.

I had received 60 letters from Helen and some cards and gifts. I wrote:

Helen, I will be back in a year. Don't worry about me, keep your letters flying. I will try to write. I received two nice letters from you and one from Mother and Dad. I tried to call home tonight, but there was a three-hour delay in Kansas City, so I cancelled it. I will try to get up at 4 in the morning to try again.

We were issued 80 rounds of ammunition. We were lying around waiting to go somewhere to meet our sea bags.

The Red Cross gave us a sack. It had a package of cigarettes, a deck of cards, a book, sewing kit, package of gum, face soap, shoe shine rag, stationery and a pencil. It was really nice of them. I gave the cigarettes to whoever wanted them.

March 10

Dearest Helen,

I had cherry pie and ice cream for supper, your favorite dessert, but I would rather see you than have a cherry pie as big as a wash-tub and 100 gallons of ice cream.

We won't get paid until we get on ship, and I think that will be soon. I hate to leave you, but I will be back soon to get you.

I got up at 4:30 a.m. to call home; it took 10 minutes to get through. We are still restricted to the barracks. I guess it won't be long now. The sergeants gave us a lecture on what to do when we get on ship, and we had lessons on bugle calls on the ship, and what pranks will be played on us (like go up top and unlock the Golden Gate). I have a round-way ticket, I hope. I believe I have.

We will get our hair cut short again — real short, and we will go to school on the ship and be on the alert for a submarine. We will eat two times a day and take a shower every other day. They told us we would be on a fast convoy and there wouldn't be much danger. (There was one ship and we zig-zagged) — it was fast. We were told what to do if we got seasick, and they told us to call the windows portholes. When we were going up on top, to say we were going topside, and when we go down, to say we were going below.

The letters Helen wrote to me March 11 through the 24th were returned to her, present address unknown.

Aboard U.S.S. Mount Vernon, California to New Caledonia, 3-11-43 to 3-25-43

MARCH 11, 1943 — We got aboard the U.S.S. Mount Vernon about 2 p.m. We pulled out of the San Diego harbor about 1 p.m. March 12. We had roll call at 9 a.m. every day and had a boat drill at 1:30 p.m. We always had a blackout on ship at sunset. No smoking was allowed on deck. We crossed the equator on the 6th or 7th day and had good weather most of the way. I had a headache, and my stomach felt funny, but I didn't get seasick. I saw flying fish and jelly fish on the way. The ocean was as blue as ink. I didn't know there was so much water! The U.S.S. Mount Vernon previously was a luxury liner which had been converted to a troop ship. It had wooden rails, and everyone carved his name in the railings.

When we first got on the ship, we were talking about how long we might be gone. I thought maybe one year. How wrong I was! I received two letters while aboard ship. They were written March 3rd and 4th. I wrote a short note to Helen saying that I was okay and feeling fine, and told her my letters would be censored from now on, and I wouldn't be able to tell where I am or what I'm doing. I told her to let my folks know she heard from me.

New Caledonia, 3-26-43 to 10-4-43

I ARRIVED AT Noumea, New Caledonia, Thursday, March 25th, and went ashore the 26th. We came to the Marine Air Base, where a camp was set up for new arrivals.

French people live here, and it is really hot. The mosquitoes were thick and big. You kill one, and 600 come to his funeral. I believed they even had teeth; we slept under nets.

I wrote to Helen March 31st. I wasn't able to tell her where I was, but I did tell her I would send a mosquito, but they were too big to get in an envelope. I asked her if she was going to get a job in town this summer. On the envelope I sent was stamped: "The Marines Have Landed," and it was free mail. I really feel lost because I don't get letters every day, and I don't get to write very often.

They sent us to the dock and we unloaded supplies (while unloading, we broke into a box or two of candy bars) and everything coming into the island off several ships for several nights, all night long. By that time we were mad enough and tired enough to join something — anything.

Our colonel talked to us about the Marine Raiders. He told us a story about a guy getting up on a high tower and staying up there until he decided to jump. He asked us if we wanted to live forever. Red Lindsay and I had gone to the meeting, but we didn't join right then. We went back to camp and talked it over. Then Red

**Left
James Singley,
Green City, Mo.**

**Right:
Joe Bibby,
Dallas, Texas.**

asked me if I thought we could pass the physical, and I said, "Let's give it a try." We joined about an hour after the talk.

It was April 2nd when Red and I joined the Marine Raiders and moved to St. Louis Camp on New Caledonia. I went in to H Company, and Red went into G Company of the 2nd Marines. We went on a small hike April 3rd.

Monday, April 5th, It has been raining every day for the past week. I went swimming in a river about two miles away, and I picked some green oranges about a mile from camp. Tuesday the mess hall caught on fire about 10:30; we put it out before it burned down.

I got acquainted with James Singley in H Company from Green City, Mo. — also Joe Bibby in G Company from Dallas, Texas. Bibby and I were good friends for a couple of months, then he came back to the States to join the Marine Air Corps. Singley was in the 3rd Squad with W.J. Russel, Neil Morley, Lloyd Luke, P.B. Noland, "Filthy" Flynn, Emil Slobodzian, Doyle Bartley, Spencer Reed and De Pung. Singley carried a BAR on Bougainville, Guam, Emirau and Okinawa.

Helen's letters that were written April 6th through May 3rd were returned to her, "present address unknown." I didn't have much time to write, but I wrote a V-mail letter on April 13th and sent Helen my new address.

April 30

My Dearest Darling Helen,

We still haven't received any mail; we must be lost where no one knows where. I go swimming some and go to a show. We had to build our own seats and stools, so I built a chair. We have outdoor shows.

Ray, in chair he built to sit in at the show.

I have seen some oxen, and they grow bananas, oranges and coconuts here. The native women work hard. They carry loads of wood on their backs, and they go barefooted.

We go on all-day hikes and eat field rations. We went up some big mountains, and a big boulder rolled down one of the mountains we were climbing. It just missed some of the men, and it scared us.

I swim in a small stream that is about 10 feet deep. There is a bank 25 or 30 feet high that we dive off. After working on the new camp today, I went swimming.

I talked to a French man the other day. He works at a saw mill and makes five francs a day; that is 12-1/2 cents in American money. He eats a piece of bread for breakfast, rice for dinner and supper.

I got into a fight with a boy (Saunders) yesterday over where I wanted to hang my clothes.

April 25th, Easter Sunday, I had to wash clothes, so I didn't go to church. I washed them in a stream and then went swimming. I

Camp Allard — 1943

was on an island that I had never studied in school, and I was tan from working in the sun.

April 29th, it rained for three days and nights. It flooded us out of our tents. So we moved to higher ground. Almost all of us had dysentery. It is muddy. We are still working on the new camp. About 800 of the old Raiders came in yesterday. They were the Raiders who had fought on Guadalcanal. There were 800 of them left out of 1100. Among those were Norman Korsmeyer (Norm), Russell Tratebas (Rusty), Thor Thostenson (later killed in action on Iwo Jima), Kenneth Frantz, Stuart Campbell (later killed in action on Bougainville), R.D. McDowell, and R.J. Spath (Richie). They joined our squad to make up 10 men. The rest of us were Bill Carroll, Ray Strohmeyer (Tex) and me. We, the new Raiders, were replacements for the Raiders who were killed, injured or sick. Thor and Frantz were good boxers.

The sun is shining bright today. We moved to the new camp that we had been working on, setting up tents and a camp for the old Raiders. It is called Camp Allard. It is built between a stream and a canal. The canal was built by the natives from upstream down to the St. Louis Mission. We tapped into the canal for our water.

My Dearest Sweetheart,

Helen, I really miss you a lot. Tell everyone "hello" for me. Honey, I want you to have a good time, but be good and I will do the same. Do you still take piano lessons? Are you going to work in town this summer? Is June in the infantry? Ask Mil if she remembers our American History teacher, "Old Man Cornwell," and tell her I don't know who my old girlfriend's mother is that works with her. Tell me, Helen, who it is.

May 3rd, I sent some roses to my mother for Mother's Day.

May 10th, I received a V-mail letter from Helen. It was written April 23rd, and was the first mail I had received for two months.

My Dearest Helen,

I am writing by candlelight and can hardly see. We don't have anything over here but will live through it.

Over the next 11 days I received five letters and two V-mails from Helen dated March 7th through the 28th, two letters from

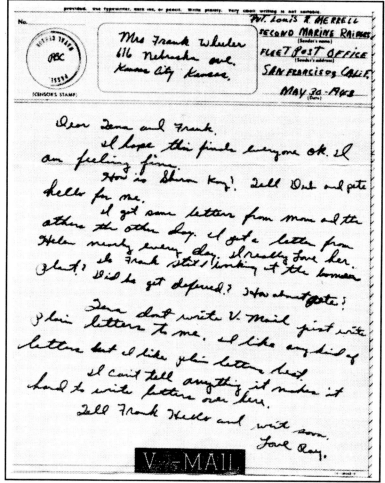

V-mail letter sent to my sister Ernie

home, and one from my sis, Ernie, in Kansas City. Robert Lindsay is telling everyone that I go "ape" when I get a letter from Helen.

Some time around the 15th of May some sergeants and corporals went up into the hills on New Caledonia to go deer hunting. One of them was in some bushes and making some noise, and the others thought it was a deer. He was shot and killed. There was no more deer hunting on New Caledonia.

One night I went to town and got some French bread and some sardines.

May 24

Dearest Helen,

We started our schedule for training, and we have school. We had to swim 100 yards and stay under water 15 seconds, float 10 seconds and tread water 15 seconds, for a second-class swimmer. We are training hard, and I don't have much time to write. I have received three letters written April 20th, May 3rd and May 4th.

I wonder, does Mr. Wilson still go with Miss Jackson (high school teachers)? That was quite a romance.

The moon is really bright and pretty here in the South Pacific shining across the ocean. It makes me homesick. I wish I could see it back in Missouri with you.

May 27th, I received two letters dated March 5th and the 8th. I wish I could hear some Boogie Woogie music; it would sound good out here.

May 29th, Artie Shaw and his band were at our camp. It was a good show; he played some popular songs. I love the song, "You Are Always in My Heart."

May 29

My Dearest Darling Helen,

Oh boy! I'm really happy now. I received four letters written May 10th, 11th, 12th and 13th.

June 1st, I started working in the mess hall for the month of June. Two or three of us peeled 45 gallons of potatoes, diced 5 gallons of carrots and peeled 15 gallons of beets by hand for one meal for 1,000 men. We get better things to eat since we have our camp built.

June 3rd, I received four letters written April 16 through 18th and three V-mail letters.

My Dearest Darling,

I am trying to take care of myself and keep in good health while I can. I am writing by lantern light. It is better than candlelight, and I can see fairly good. I'm glad you are helping Viola and your folks this summer instead of working in town.

June 8 — I received two letters dated May 22nd and 24th.

My Dearest Helen,

I am writing on a little stand I built out of a few boxes. It isn't

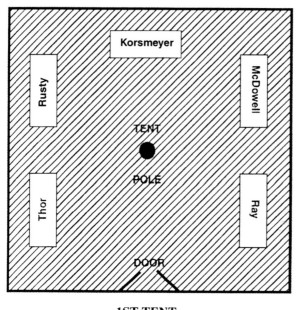

1ST TENT

1st Tent (5 men of 10-man squad).

In second tent — the other five men: Spath, Carroll, Strohmeyer, Frantz and Campbell. Each man slept under individual mosquito nets. We built a square around the tent pole to put our things on. We have dirt floors, so we built a floor under the square to put our seabags on. We put our clothes under our mattress to press them. Lister bags with four spigots were filled with water from a canal coming out of the mountains for drinking water. It was flavored with chlorine.

Above is a diagram of our tent. Our 10-man squad was divided into two tents.

---

very good, but it serves the purpose. The mosquitoes are bothering me; they really get on your nerves after so long.

I see Red Lindsay about every day, but I don't get to run around with him any more. We are in different companies. Spath and I go

**Left:
Ray Merrell,
movie screen
in
background.**

**Right:
Richie Spath**

TEN-MAN SQUAD

Left to right: Rusty Tratebas, Thor Thostenson (KIA Iwo Jima), Norm Korsmeyer, R.D. McDowell, Ray (Tex) Strohmeyer, Ray Merrell.

Kenneth Frantz and Richie Spath

Bill Carroll

Stuart Campbell (KIA Bougainville)

to boxing matches to see Thor and Franz box, and we play volley-ball. Lindsay and I play horseshoes. He has played a lot and is an excellent player. Red is married and has a little girl four years old.

Meanwhile, back in Marshall, Mo., the Missouri Valley College was turned into a Reserve Officers Training Camp (ROTC), and the Navy came to town, with their sharp white uniforms and jaunty white hats.

In our rare spare time about ten of us made 30 gallons of cherry jack. We used six gallons of cherries, 20 pounds of sugar and some yeast. It fermented in 8 to 10 days in the South Pacific heat. Pretty strong stuff! I had been on guard duty at the food warehouse one night from 8 p.m. until midnight. About 11 p.m. some guys came. One carried the six gallons of cherries and the others the 20 pounds

Ray Merrell

*Left:
with
45-caliber
pistrol.*

of sugar. We made the 30 gallons of booze in a wooden barrel.

June 24th — I was issued a 45-caliber Thompson machine gun (Tommy gun) and a K-Bar knife USMC. I turned in my M-1 rifle.

Helen writes that her sister Mil, Ed and Dotty are back to Missouri from Connecticut. Helen is driving her dad's car sometimes.

On June 30th I received a letter from my sister Norma in Hamilton, one from my brother Nelson, and a card from Helen. I sent Helen a hankie a little girl 11 years old had embroidered New Caledonia and some other stuff on it. I also sent her a ring I had made out of a U.S. silver quarter. I made myself one out of a half-dollar. I had just a small hammer and hatchet, and it took me about 12 hours, but I just worked on it when I had time.

I have been going to a movie each night and have seen "Shepherd of the Hills," "Once Upon a Honeymoon," "The Black Swan" and "A Yank on the Burma Road."

July 1st we started training again. We went into the fields and had combat practice. We had inspections of clothes, bunk and personal appearance. We took turns with guard duty, went on hikes, had night problem practice, ambush practice and school on marksmanship. We would strip down our weapons and put them back together and

John E. Cosmos in camouflage suit with Tommy gun.

had working parties where we cleaned the camp and unloaded trucks. We were issued our Raider boots and camouflage suits.

Some of the guys fired rounds of rifle and machine gun fire out in the ocean, celebrating the 4th of July. No one got into trouble. I cleaned out my seabag, washed clothes and swam. I slept until noon Sunday.

On the 5th I received letters from Helen written June 14th and 15th, one from Dad and one from Cora Lea. My dad's mother died, and he didn't get to go to the funeral because of high water. My brother Paul's birthday was yesterday. He is working for Municipal Utilities in Marshall, Mo. and is now 23. I had guard duty of the mess hall this evening from 8 to 12.

Ray Merrell with Raider boots on.

We had clothes inspection and signed up for new ones. We soak our clothes in a bucket of water and soap, use a brush on them, then take them to a mountain stream to rinse them.

Headquarters put on a show, trying to entertain us. It was fairly good. Then Spath and I played volleyball; he won. The next day we went on a hike, then we played two more games of volleyball, and I won both. I went to the fights last night at Camp Gretchen. The 3rd Raiders fought, and two fights were won by knockouts.

I haven't heard many of the songs on the Hit Parade, but I enjoy reading the songs that are popular now. The songs we sing over here are "Show Me the Way to Go Home," or something we make up that fits us over here.

I went to Noumea with Chaplain McCorkle to get a piano. The different companies get up skits and put on shows.

We had school mornings and went into the field in the afternoon. We had night problems and had inspections.

It isn't so hot here now. It is supposed to be winter, but the natives are just planting their gardens, so I guess it's spring. It starts getting hot here when it's cold in the States.

We hiked up mountains, had field problems and rubber boat training. I fell in the water, and we all got wet. We raided an island for practice. The next day we got up at 2:30 a.m. and went to the ocean and raided three little islands around this one for practice. We had lots of inspections.

I received five letters from Helen, five letters from my sisters and brothers and Mom and Dad. I guess I heard from everyone I love. All the letters were written between June 16th and the 21st. When I don't get a letter, I just say the ship isn't in with the mail.

I went to Noumea with Morley, Bibby, Russell and Gonzales. We had supper in town.

I had received over 60 letters from Helen since being across. I told her to have a good time, and I will come back to you as soon as I can.

We get all we want of gum and candy at the PX now.

July 20th I received four letters from Helen and several from home. James Chambers joined the Navy. Before he went to Colorado, he wanted me to join the Merchant Marines, but he left, so here I am, and I like it, too.

July 26th I received five letters from Helen and one from my sister Mildred.

My Dear Helen,

Don't worry about me. I am safe, I think. When you don't get a letter, then you know I am fighting. I will always write as much as I can.

I saw a good movie, "This Above All." I thought it was very good.

Some days we are out on the firing range all day. We take turns having guard duty, and we are still going out on field problems with the platoon in attack. One day on working detail we rolled up 30 rubber boats. We had school on marksmanship, studied our weapons and stripped them. General Vandergrift inspected the troops on July 30th.

August 1

Dearest Darling Helen,

I received a letter several days ago, but I haven't had time to write. I enjoy reading the names of the songs that are popular in the States now. I hear a few of them, when they play records at the show area before the show. I received three letters from home.

August 8th — I slipped a piece of French money in an envelope after the other letter had been censored and told Helen on

**French money that Ray slipped in envelope
after the letter had been censored.**

the money that I had been on New Caledonia all the time, but would soon be leaving for action. I told her I came across on the U.S.S. Mount Vernon, and I told her to make up a code for islands and China of some good sentences and send me a copy.

I made PFC, August 4, 1943.

August 13th — I received 10 letters from Helen. They were written July 14 through the 27th, and I received two letters from home.

Dearest Sweetheart,

I am in a safe place, so don't worry. There will be times I won't get to write for two or three months. I would love to be with you in your peaceful front yard with nothing to worry about. In the picture you sent, it looks like there is a lot of white clover in your yard. You know I love you. I hope you don't fall in love with any of the Navy boys at home.

**Helen, with white
clover in front yard.**

I still do my own laundry, and I am getting tired of doing it, but I will live through it. We had feet and dog tag inspections and went swimming with our clothes on to qualify by swimming 50 yards. We threw hand grenades to practice.

I got a letter from Lora Lee and one from Dorothy.

Colonel Shapley gave us a talk on August 9th. We loaded the rubber boats into a truck and went after K rations, then went out in the woods to practice attack. The next day we put the rubber boats in the ocean and went to a little island to stay overnight. The water was extremely rough. We got up at 5 a.m. and had guard duty on the island. We were back to camp at 3 p.m.

On the 14th we had another inspection by General Vandergrift. On the 17th we drew equipment, a coat, a canvas bucket and pan, gas mask and a first aid packet.

Hello, Darling,

You were teasing me about the natives, so I will describe my new girlfriend to you. She is 5 foot 5 inches, and she wears pretty dresses, red, yellow, orange and a purple one, which hangs down to her pretty black feet that are size 13. She has a fanny like a camel. I share her with many other Marines. She has six husbands and 18 kids, so you can just picture that. Draw me a picture of her; I would love to see her.

We went out in the field and practiced creeping and crawling up a big hill. We stayed in the field all night and got up at 3:15 a.m. and hiked 11 miles.

We are still having guard duty and field problems and all-day trash runs.

August 16th I received five letters and a card with a picture in it from Helen. I have it posted in the book she gave me. The letters were dated from July 12th through August 3rd. I told her I am going to try to write more often while I can. Keep writing to me.

Every Sunday night Chaplain McCorkle holds a short sermon, so I go to church every Sunday night. There is a Red Cross building in Noumea. They have pool tables, table tennis and a reading and writing room and a place to get sandwiches. They also put on boxing bouts, and there is a picture show downtown for the military.

The people here dress funny. Most of the natives go barefooted. The little boys two or three years old run around the house with just a little shirt on and no pants. The native men, most of them, wear clothes that we throw away or are torn. The women wear long dresses that look like just a piece of material wrapped around them that hang to their ankles. The other few people dress like we do in the States, but not as good.

I got a letter from Cora Lea, and my folks have moved to the edge of town. I guess my dad got tired of living in town.

I can't tell when it's winter or summer here. The leaves stay on the trees all the time, but it's cooler sometimes; I guess it's winter then. The natives' gardens are small, but the peas are blooming, and the sweet corn is about eight inches high. The natives raise some rice; they plow their fields with oxen, and they are slow. It looks like the natives are pushing the oxen.

We can't see the Big Dipper in the sky. Instead we see the Southern Cross; it looks like a kite. The stars on the Raider Patch represent the Southern Cross.

The natives build the frames of their houses out of logs and strip it with bamboo; the sides and roofs are fixed with grass and don't look so bad. The white people live in houses like Americans, but some aren't as nice.

These islands aren't like the ones you see in shows, but they are pretty when you get on top of a large hill or mountain and look down on the green foothills, and the green valley where you can see the blue ocean, the shapely coconut trees, and the rice fields divided off into sections. It is a beautiful sight, but there are no pretty girls dancing around in grass skirts!

August 17th, several Marines that were veterans of the Makin Raid were celebrating the one-year anniversary of the raid. They were up in the hills and firing their rifles. One of them decided to fire over the tent of Col. Shapley. Immediately we had roll call, "as you are," in shorts, nude or whatever, to find out who was not there. George Clark was not there (the others either got

The Raider Patch. The stars represent the Southern Cross.

29

back or someone answered for them). George was put in the brig for 30 days on bread and water, or as it is called, "wine and cake."

Those of us who worked on KP at the time would hollow out the inside of a loaf of bread, put jelly and butter inside for him. We also threw apples and other fruit over the fence to him. He survived pretty well.

August 18th, Col. Shapley gave us another talk. We went out in the field and practiced creeping and crawling up a big hill. We drew ammunition for the problem.

August 24th, I received letters from Helen dated August 5th, 6th, 8th and 9th, and one from Mom and Dad.

Dearest Darling Helen,

I bet there are a lot of sailors around town now. I hope you don't fall in love with any of them and forget me.

I saw a good movie the other night. It was "Somewhere I'll Find You." I hope I find you again someday.

I really feel good today. I got up and went swimming in a cold stream before breakfast.

On New Caledonia Red and I were about 200 yards apart. We were set up in a square with a parade ground in the center. There are 250 men (one company) with five men to a tent. There were four companies: E, F, G and H.

We went swimming, washed clothes or went to a movie after working. We usually had Sundays off to write letters, play horseshoes or whatever.

September 1st, I wrote to Paul, Lora Lee and Dub (Norma).

Mrs. Eleanor Roosevelt and Lanny Ross visited our camp to entertain us. Lanny Ross sang us lots of popular songs. He was good. Mrs. Roosevelt inspected us and gave us a talk.

September 2nd I received four letters from Helen and a package from home. The letters were written August 13th, 15th, 16th and 18th. I wrote:

Dearest Helen,

I bet Mildred hates to see Eddie leave. I am still waiting for a picture of you in your bathing suit. I will never get too many pictures, so keep sending them every chance you get.

September 12th, I received four more letters from Helen. They were written August 18th, 20th, 23rd and 25th.

Hi, Dearest,

I don't have much time to write except on Sunday. The wind is blowing hard. I have my paper stuck down with thumb tacks so it won't blow away. It seems the Marine Corps doesn't give furloughs. I guess they think you can't win the war at home. I think the Marines that are drafted now get to go home. They don't have much discipline in boot camp. They get liberty and candy from the PX, and the platoon leaders can't even swear at them. They even get ranks in boot camp. There are boys in this outfit that have silver star medals that are PFC's and lots of college boys it took 16 months to make a rating, but I guess a rating isn't everything.

I'm afraid the Japs aren't going to quit like Italy did. They like to fight too well for that!

I am saving pictures of my buddies and friends, so I can fix up an album when I get home, or before.

September 16th, I wrote Helen by way of code, that we would be leaving to attack enemy bases. I wrote again on the 21st.

Hello, Honey,

I'm glad I joined the Marines. We catch hell, but that is what makes a Marine.

You said June went from California to North Carolina, and Eddie is in the Navy. Since Eddie joined the Navy, you three are the "Three Little Sisters." Mary loves a Soldier, Mildred loves a Sailor, and Helen loves a Marine (I hope)

Helen, from the bottom of my heart, I really love you, but I want you to have a good time while you are young and in high school. If you go with boys, go with them all, not just one, because you might fall in love again. I hope not.

Don't worry about me. I will al-

**Three sisters —
Mildred, Mary, Helen.**

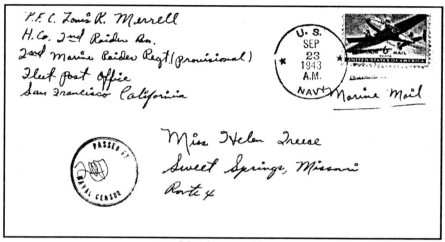

Marine mail.

ways come back to you. Be sure to have a good time. You won't ever regret it. I want you to be happy; then I will be happy.

The mosquitoes are really bad here again. I have to put up a mosquito net every night.

On September 22nd I drew a BAR (Browing Automatic Rifle). We had a fire group firing. I fired 110 rounds with my BAR; then I cleaned it. I drew a BAR belt (ammo belt). I went to the rifle range and fired 70 rounds with my BAR and got zeroed in.

September 30th, I drew ammunition for my BAR. I packed my seabag, and I loaded ammo at the Navy ammunition depot for our battalion onto the ship. I got through at 5:30 and went to bed early.

We could not write letters now.

One night we were getting ready to go back to camp after having liberty. We were loading the truck when Kenny started kidding Cecil Jenks about being a recruit. Kenny had been drinking; Jenks was built like a boxer. Kenny just kept razzing him, about that time Jenks knocked Kenny off the truck. On the ground Jenks raised his foot up in the air and said, "Am I supposed to kill him now?"

Kenny's lip was split. Back at Camp Allard, Kenny had to find Dr. Ware to sew up his lip. That was the end of the razzing.

Helen writes that she stays in town some with her brother John, Viola and Roger. John's house burned down in Mt. Leonard, and they moved to town before moving to another farm.

October 3rd, I was on a working party, but it was secured, so I went swimming this a.m., then worked unloading lumber at the docks.

U.S.S. President Hayes, 10-4-43 to 10-11-43

ON THE 4th I got up at 5 a.m. and worked all day loading ship, etc. At 4:30 p.m. we boarded the ship, the U.S.S. President Hayes. I got letters from Helen, Lora Lee, Pop and Mildred. On the 5th we lay around in the Harbor of New Caledonia all day and went to bed early. On the 6th we were still in the harbor. I rested and cleaned my BAR, then went to a show on the ship. It was "The Immortal Sergeant."

I had guard duty on the ship. The 7th we pulled out of the harbor at 2:45 p.m. I got really seasick at 1 a.m.; the sea was very rough. I had told Helen by code that "we are leaving this place — destination unknown."

We had five ships and five destroyers with us. I washed clothes. It was very hot, and I slept topside.

On October 9th we passed New Hebrides about noon. On the 10th we were getting close to Guadalcanal, and I packed my pack.

Guadalcanal, 10-11-43

WE ARRIVED AT Guadalcanal October 11th. We unloaded ship and camped out in the field. We had an air raid warning.

U.S.S. George Clymer, 10-12-43 to 10-15-43

OCTOBER 12th — We loaded the U.S.S. George Clymer with gear, and we slept in the field. We went to sea during the night of October 13th and headed for Efate, one of the New Hebrides islands. October 15th, 1943, Joe Bibby wrote to Helen:

Dear Helen,

I was in Ray's company in the 2nd Raiders until September 1st. I am back here now for the Marine Air Corps.

Ray and I were pretty close, and I can tell you this for him; he is healthy, happy (as happy as you can be, that far from home and

Joe Bibby

the girl), and he is in Noumea, New Caledonia. I didn't have to be very close to know that, did I? I can tell you he loves you a lot though. I haven't seen my girl since December '41. I'm going to Dallas now though, and if she stayed true to me all that time, I will be happier than she will ever know. She didn't write very often though the last three or four months, so I just don't know. I'm telling you this so you'll understand. If you feel you don't love him in the future, tell him so — don't keep him guessing too much. Maybe a little won't hurt, but at least write often. You're pretty swell about that though.

I'm just trying to say — he loves you like I love my girl, and she hurt me pretty bad. Maybe when I get home, everything will be okay. I hope you two get together.

Tell him you heard from me, and tell his mother where he is and how he is. Tell him to write to me.

Sincerely,
Joe Bibby

Efate, 10-15-43 to 10-23-43

ON OCTOBER 15th we pulled into the harbor of Efate, New Hebrides, a pretty island. While there, we went out in Higgins boats to time for the landing. We had a dummy run one morning at 8 a.m. in

New Hebrides Island, Efate.

Higgins boats and were back at 2 p.m. We went on a two-day problem, camped out and dug foxholes. We had outposts and stood watch.

On the 18th we were still in the harbor of Efate. We lay around all day.

We were back on the ship on the 22nd. We had swiped a 50-gallon barrel of wine from the French, and had a little wine party.

Efate, beautiful island.

U.S.S. George Clymer, 10-23-43 to 10-27-43

OCTOBER 23rd — We pulled out of Efate on the way back to Guadalcanal. We stopped at Espiritu Santo for two days. On the 25th we pulled out of Santo to go to Guadalcanal.

Guadalcanal, 10-27-43

OCTOBER 27th — We arrived on Guadalcanal and picked up mail. We were there one night. I had been unable to write letters for one month and 25 days. I wrote Helen a V-mail letter. I told her by code that I was on Guadalcanal, and for her to tell my folks she heard from me.

U.S.S. George Clymer — 10-28-43 to 11-1-43

OCTOBER 28th, 29th and 30th — We were on our way to Bougainville. I received several letters from Helen. They were written September 7th, 10th, 12 and 14th. It's impossible to answer them now. It is really hot here.

Somewhere in the South Pacific — undated
Dearest Darling Helen,
I have been busy, and letters have been coming in, so I'm behind in writing. I have lost a few pounds. I try to live clean over here while I can. I also try to be happy; that is rather hard to do without you. The guys crack a few jokes, and we listen to each other's stories, but our morale gets very low at times. Your letters pep me up. I have learned to appreciate things I had at home that I didn't think about having before, but I think of them now.
I haven't heard your favorite song, "Sunday, Monday or Always."

October 31st I stood gun watch. I manned an anti-aircraft gun 12 midnight until 4 a.m. on the U.S.S. George Clymer. It was cloudy and raining. We were getting close to Bougainville.

Bougainville, 11-1-43 to 1-12-44

Going to the front on the Piva trail.

NOVEMBER 1st — We made the beachhead at Empress Augusta Bay, Bougainville. We hit the beach at 7 a.m. Col. Joe McCaffery and several others were killed on the beach. We pushed in 300 yards. Rev. William McCorkle was hit on the helmet, but wasn't injured. The bullet went through the helmet and lining and grazed his head just a little. He wanted to keep the helmet, so the Seabees welded the holes shut.

The next day we pushed in 500

Ray Merrell with BAR and a pal.

more yards.

November 3rd I was able to write Helen a short letter.

November 4th a friend (Work) was shot in the leg. It was a worrisome night.

We held the beachhead the next four days, then went to the Piva Trail road block. We went up the trail early in the day.

About 3 p.m. the corporals and lieutenants wanted us to dig new foxholes, but some of the old Raiders (Russell, Thor, Spath, Korsmeyer and Tratebas) said, "We better get our ass in gear before the Japs hit." The Japs hit us about 4:30 p.m. We had a hot fire fight. I was carrying a BAR (automatic rifle).

One Marine came through our lines. He had been shot in the mouth. His teeth and lips were just hanging. He said to us, "Isn't this a hell of a way to go home?"

It started to rain and rained all night. It filled our old foxholes, and it was like a sea of water. We were in the water-filled foxholes for 16 hours. When the Japs fired their knee mortars, we would duck under the water. Sgt. Ignatius Gorak was killed during the night, and several boys were wounded.

November 8th at daylight Capt. Robert Burnett told Lt. Skip Daly to send out a squad of 10 men to see what was out in front of us. The H Company, Squad 2, was Thor Thostenson, R.D. McDowell, Norm Korsmeyer, Rusty Tratebas, Kenneth Frantz, Richie Spath, Ray Strohmeyer, Stuart Campell, Bill Carroll and me.

We got out about 10 to 25 yards, and the Japs pinned us down with rifle and machine gun fire.

We came back and told Lt. Daly, and he told Capt. Burnett. The captain in-

Russell on the Piva Trail.

Thor Thostenson

structed Lt. Daly to take his platoon (three squads including ours) and make contact with the Japs. Lt. Daly fired a burst at a Jap with his carbine rifle. Then all hell broke loose. We passed over several dead Japs. We got out about 200 to 300 yards, and the Japs hit us with mortar and machine gun fire.

I didn't see the Jap that was firing at me. I was moving pretty fast. I got in a small ravine, and my BAR ammo belt got caught on a vine. I pulled so hard it pulled one of the ammo pockets loose.

Stuart Campbell out of our squad was killed by mortar. Kenneth Frantz of our squad was bounced off the ground by the same mortar fire.

We were reinforced by F and G Companies, including Red Lindsay and two Lang brothers from Joplin, Mo.

Our H Company pulled back at 4 p.m. to set up a line in the rear. Then we pulled back to a swamp area and rested on logs to keep out of the water. We slept in the swamps. We had been at the roadblock on the Piva Trail for 24 hours.

The next day, November 9, we started back to the front in mud up to our knees and butt. There were a lot of wounded boys during the night, and they were bringing out the wounded Marines. Bob Seaman from Beardstown, Ill. was one of the wounded. Just before we got to the front, the fighting quieted down. We (H Company) pulled back off the lines to a rest area.

Stuart Campbell's grave on Bougainville.

The other three companies, F, G and E, stayed on the front. Many boys were wounded from our battalion (four companies).

Per Rusty's letter dated February 27th, 1985: "The picture of Rainbow's (Stuart Campbell) grave brought back memories. It's a wonder any of us got back from that patrol."

November 8th I received some pictures of Helen. I wrote her a V-mail letter with a pencil about an inch long. I only had one piece of paper to write on, but told her I would have more in a few days if I had time to write.

November 13th, I wrote a letter to Helen, the first time since October 27th, on Red Cross stationery.

I received several letters from her and my folks. I really enjoyed them, as usual. I told her I was feeling fine, although I had lost a little weight. I told her by code that I was fighting on Bougainville. I wrote the letter sitting behind a big tree. I told her I couldn't answer all her questions right now, but will some day, and that I would write every chance I got, but that wouldn't be very often. I wrote:

Bartley, Spencer, Slobodzian, Flynn, Russell, after the battle.

I hope you received the three V-mails. That was just to let you know I was okay, and I still think of you. I will write when I can. Remember I will always love you. Three more days have passed, and I'm still okay. I sure hated it that I couldn't write to you and my folks, but this is part of the war. It is getting dark, so will quit for now. Please excuse this old beat-up paper, but you know how things are, I hope. I'm glad you heard from Joe Bibby. He's a swell guy.

November 16th, I wrote that Bibby's girlfriend (Mary Anne) was about to get married. He made it home just in time; they are engaged now. He had gone with her three years before joining the Marines. He fought on Makin and Guadalcanal and was in the Marines 18 months before going back to the States for the Marine Air Force.

November 17th, Trigger Wall was disassembling a rifle grenade, and it exploded. My squad leader, Thor Thostenson, got lots of pieces and had to be evacuated by ship. Trigger had two fingers blown off. I had several pieces in my chest. The corpsmen dug them out; they were just under the skin. I had just gotten down in my foxhole to get a drink of water, and Thor kneeled down in front of me, saying he wanted a drink, too. It was at that time the grenade went off. Thor got most of it. Trigger Wall got the nickname "Trigger" because he was trigger happy. He would shoot at the least little sound. He carried explosives in his seabag and was always checking out different kinds of explosives.

On the 18th I got a Jap skull and an arm bone for my K-Bar knife. I gave the skull to Spath to bring home when he came back to the States.

November 20th, we went back up to the front lines in the hills.

Washing up in the Piva Trail stream.

During the night of the 22nd, Spath was at the top of the hill. Vines were attached to him and others on guard duty in the lower area. The vine broke, so he threw dirt clods at me to keep me awake. The clods would ricochet off our shelter halves and go down to the next foxhole, etc. The Marines at the foot of the hill didn't know what was going on.

Later that night Spath got sick and was evacuated. I was on watch. Strohmeyer turned in his Tommy gun and carried Spath's BAR.

Cantral, Trigger Wall, Frantz.

We made an 800-yard push through the jungle the next day. Strohmeyer wasn't used to the BAR, and he took his thumb off safety and it started firing. He didn't know how to stop it. When it started firing, he was so excited he couldn't tell us he was the one firing. No one was injured. Armin H. Miester was killed during the night.

We had a handful of turkey on the evening of the 24th. Thanksgiving Day, November 25th, we had a little turkey to eat on the front lines. On the 26th we had a helmet full of turkey for ten men (our squad), and it tasted good.

November 28th — We came off the front lines to a rest area. I was happy that I was feeling good and still able to write and receive letters.

November 29th — We got back to our camping area, and we had mail there. I was lucky. I had several letters from Helen and my folks. I really enjoyed them, believe me! I had received 14 letters from Helen since I left New Caledonia. I had them all, so I would try to answer all her questions while I had a little time.

Ray Strohmeyer.

Dearest Helen,

I don't get a chance to write often, but I still think of you lots. Nelson told me Curtis is in the Navy Seabees. Robert Lindsay is still with me. I see him about every week.

The Red Cross gave us some paper, gum, playing cards, cigarettes, soap, pencil and a sewing kit. It comes in handy on this deserted island.

I am sending a picture of Bibby and me. He sent it to me; it's been wet. I was a little fat then, but I've lost it all now.

I really love the pictures you sent me. I look at them all the time. It's hard to keep pictures out there; it's so damp, and it rains every day. I feel fine and am happy I am still able to write and get your letters. Do you ever think of us getting married in a few years? I think of you as my future wife.

December 2

Dearest Darling,

While I am resting, I will try to write. It is raining, but I have a shelter. I don't feel so good today. I guess I'm getting run down after so long, but I'll feel better in a few days, I hope.

December 3rd, two of us carried a roll of barbed wire (80#), up to the front lines through mud up to our knees. The barbed wire was on a pole. We went up a steep hill, so had to hold the pole up to keep it from sliding down to one end. We grabbed tree sprouts or whatever to pull up the hill (30 men carried 15 rolls). We had spotted a place to swim on the way up. So after the two of us delivered

Ray Merrell and Joe Bibby.

our barbed wire to the front line, we went swimming.

Lt. Skip Daly didn't know where we were, but when he found out, he put the two of us on KP duty at headquarters for 17 days, until December 20th (that may be the best thing that ever happened to me). One Japanese plane usually bombed us every night at headquarters, but I wasn't on the front line. I wrote a V-mail letter because I didn't have any envelopes. I received two letters from Helen written October 19th and November 17th. That's the latest I have gotten.

Helen

December 11th was my 21st birthday. I received two letters from Helen dated November 11th and 14th and one from my folks.

My Dearest Helen,

I'll try to find an envelope so I can mail this. It's my birthday. I believe I feel my age; I feel older than I would have if I hadn't gotten in the service. I have been through lots of hell and worried quite a bit, but still out for a good time when I get home.

Tell Mary and June and your mother and dad "hello" for me.

I remember when some of the old bunch of kids we used to run around with used to tell about your dad not liking for some boy to take you home, but I can see why. You were a little young. I thought a lot of you even then, but to get back to the subject, was I scared to meet your dad because of that! Gee! He wasn't half bad; he always treated me okay. He was a lot of fun. I remember the night the three of us played cards. Your mother was always cheerful and always treated me swell. I always seemed at home when I was out there in the good old peaceful country under a big shade tree.

About a month ago I had a feeling I wouldn't get to see my 21st birthday, but I did, so I was fooled.

Mom told me Nelson didn't get into the Merchant Marines because of his ear. He probably wants in the service, but he doesn't know what it's like and what you go through. I know the Marines catch "hell and high water," but I still like it here.

I hope you get this letter for Christmas, and I hope you like what my sis, Mildred, picked out for you — for me.

December 13

My Dearest Sweetheart,

Robert Lindsay's wife has been going with some soldier and is going to have a child from him. I feel sorry for him. He has been married six years and has a little girl four or five years old. His wife has sold everything he had. I am still with him. He is in G Company and I'm in H Company. I see him quite a bit now. If you write to his aunt, you can tell her where he has been with me.

It seems we are not so close to each other as we were, but it's because I couldn't write and it takes longer for me to get your letters, but I still love to get them. I just saw two bags of mail, so I might get a letter from you — I hope so. I can hardly wait now.

Do you feel bad because I came into your life? If something does happen to me, you are still young and mighty pretty. But I'll be back someday, darling, just you wait and see.

Mom told me about Bobby McDonough getting deferred. I bet he's a hell of a farmer! He is also getting married.

I would love to have some good old-fashioned eggs and some good old-fashioned milk, instead of powdered milk and eggs, but I am thankful for what we have out here.

I received three letters dated November 18th, 20th and 22nd, and a birthday card with a letter in it.

Hello, Helen,

Well, I just finished the letters I received. I read them over three or four times, and the birthday card with a letter in it. Helen, we are still plenty close, because I feel you in my heart now and forever and ever. I am very happy now.

December 19

My Dearest Sweetheart,

It's nearly Christmas, but it doesn't seem like it to me. Have many gas stations closed since rationing? Can you still get hamburgers and hot dogs at lunch stands? What about ice cream? What are the popular songs now? Are many of the girls going steady with the sailors? Are any getting married? Is Shorty Pace overseas?

They are having church now, but I couldn't go. I am on guard. We cleaned off a small place for church outside. I went to the church last Sunday. Everyone out here needs someone to put your beliefs in and to share some of your troubles with. I know I have found it useful and am closer to Him.

Please write when you can.

December 21st, we went back to the front lines. An apron of barbed wire was stretched like an A frame with a machine gun on each end to keep the Japs from coming through. We had patrols and guard duty at the outpost, looking out over the cane fields.

Our platoon of 30 men went on a 3500-yard patrol through jungle and swamps. We had two Doberman Pincer dogs. We left at 6 a.m. and were back at 4:30 p.m. Our own planes started to bomb us, so we set up a portable radio (we had to crank it to get the generator started, and it made a lot of noise) to tell them to quit bombing. We got back without anyone getting injured.

I had Mom and Mildred pick out a watch for Helen for Christmas.

> *From an isle down south*
> *an' a long ways west,*
> *I send you Season's Wishes*
> *for the best.*
> *I send my love*
> *and thoughts sincere,*
> *I send my hopes*
> *for the coming year.*
> *I'll breathe a prayer*
> *for a Nation Free,*
> *and I hope next Christmas*
> *I can send you ME.*

Merry Christmas
1943
from the 2nd Marine
Raider Battalion.

December 25

Dearest Helen (Terry),

I got a letter from you last night dated November 27th; it was a nice Christmas present. I also received the Easter card you sent me, but it had the same meaning. I received four or five old letters from my folks and one from my sis, Mildred. We didn't get our Christmas packages. They have been stored away for a month or two; that's what they tell us anyway. I hope you sent me a picture. I hope you had a Merry Christmas and a happy one. I am happy because I am still able to write.

I'm sitting out in the morning sun sweating. I have my shirt off, getting a little more sun if that's possible. Perspiration is dripping off my elbows. As the sun shines through the thick trees and vines, it knocks off some of the heat, but it's still hot. We are just a few degrees from the equator. Did you have a white Christmas?

We had an earthquake yesterday morning. It really shook the trees and ground. The ground just rolled under your feet. You could feel it all day, but just slightly. There is a volcano on the island. It puts out a huge smoke all the time. It's about a mile away. I have to be on alert now so will sign off.

December 26th, Jim Trent (Henry Rawlings' buddy) was wounded, and on the 27th Kelso and Charles Cain were killed.

New Year's night I stood guard when it was my turn. I slept in a foxhole.

January 5, 1944

My Dearest Helen,

I started a letter about six or seven days ago, but I didn't have time to finish it. We received our Christmas packages January 3rd. My buddies and I enjoyed the can of candy you sent. Thanks a million for the swell knife and chain, and thanks for the film. I received several nice presents from my folks and lots of candy. I hope you like your watch; the note was straight from my heart. I received a letter from James Chambers and one from Shorty Pace. Shorty's letter was dated May 5th. Jimmy is engaged to Ola H., who lives in Miami, Mo. He asked about you. He told me to hang on to you because you were really okay, but I already knew that.

I can tell you now that I made the beachhead on Bougainville. I am okay, so you don't have to worry. I don't have much time to write now days. I promise a long letter as soon as I have time.

When I first met you, I knew I would love to go with you. I remember seeing you at Bernard's Lunch and at the Spot. Do you remember when you used to be in the Spot with some other girls? Did you ever notice me looking at you all the time? I was just wishing I could go with you. You just broke my heart, the first time you were playing the piano at Margie's house. I fell for you and wanted to kiss you, but we were both with someone else.

I really enjoyed coming out to your house because your mother and dad were so nice to me.

One of the guys in our platoon wanted to heat some water in a canteen cup. He had some 30's and 50's tracer bullets, so he took the point of the bullets out of the casing. He took a pocket knife and dug the powder loose from two bullets. He set the canteen cup on the casing part of the shells and lit the tracer powder. He was happy when the water started to boil, but then the casings exploded and made two holes in his canteen cup.

January 11th, 1944, we were relieved on the front line by the Army. We camped out overnight by the Marine Drive (built by our good friends, the Seabees).

At 10:30 on the 12th we hiked to the beach to get aboard ship, the U.S.S. Hayes, to leave Bougainville. We had established the beachhead on Bougainville November 1st, 1943, and fought on the island 73 days. We built pillboxes and strung aprons of barbed wire.

U.S.S. President Hayes, 1-12-44 to 1-13-44

We boarded the U.S.S. President Hayes at 11:30 January 12th, and we pulled away at 5 p.m. We rested on the ship; we didn't even get shot at.

It took 24 hours to get to Guadalcanal. We pulled in at 5 p.m. and stayed on the ship overnight.

Guadalcanal, 1-14-44 to 3-17-44

We were off the ship at 9:30 a.m. January 14th. We had working parties on the beach (unloading) and put up tents in the rain. It really rained.

On the 15th the wind blew down a coconut tree that fell on the bunk of Phillip Calalano and killed him. The tree was weak from naval gunfire that had gone through the tree when the Marines landed there in 1942, and also from the rain-soaked ground.

Ray on Guadalcanal Beach

Hi, Sweetheart,

At last I have time to answer your letters. I had a good night's sleep and feel fine today. It seems good to be able to write and not be worried about something while doing so.

My buddies and I really enjoyed the candy you sent. I sure hope you don't get tired waiting for me

Left: Ray with lister bag for drinking water on the left, barrel for trash.

I told Helen in code that I was on Guadalcanal again. I wrote:

The thoughts of you helped me through thick and thin. I saw Mary's picture in the paper; she sure looks a lot like you. I bet you enjoy working at Missouri Valley stores. That's a swell place. I received your New Year's card. I want to wish you a Happy Birthday. I wish I could send you a nice card and gift, but I'll be thinking of you. Another good night's sleep or two and I should feel good again.

January 20
Dearest Sweetheart,
I received your long and very sweet letter of January 2nd. Mildred sent me some photograph albums, and I fixed all your pictures in it. I look at them all the

Ray and Robert Lindsay

time. It's really hot here today. I wish I were under a big shade tree in your front yard; I bet it's rather cool there now. I've heard several of the new songs you told me about. Did you like "Pistol Packin' Mama"?

We set up a new camp and then we rested. My tent is about fifty yards from the ocean.

I feel fine and healthy, as far

Left: Red Lindsay with Japanese rifle and Japanese automatic rifle.

as I know. My feet are better now. I hope I'm in this good of condition when I get back. It's fairly hot here; the ocean breeze helps a little, and our camp is in a coconut grove so we have a little shade. I just got back from taking a swim and bath in a fresh water stream. It's about a mile from here, but I caught a ride. I don't care so much about swimming in the ocean because it's so

Ray Merrell with Japanese rifle and Japanese automatic rifle

salty. Sometimes I just stand on the beach and gaze toward the east.

Robert Lindsay and I tried to get transferred to anything to get off the front lines, but no luck. We did get into the heavy weapons company. Being on a 37MM tank gun was a little better risk.

January 23rd I received two letters from Helen. The letters were written December 29th and the 31st.

My Darling Helen,

I really love your letters. I couldn't get along without them. I'm sitting here on my bunk writing.

Yes, darling, Mr. and Mrs. Alderman are really swell people to work for. I used to work for them when I was about 16. I went to Maryville, Missouri with her and stayed three or four days one time to help with her mother's estate sale.

Who gave you the nickname Terry?

January 28th, I received a letter written January 5th.

Ray Merrell on the beach, Guadalcanal.

Robert Lindsay,
Guadalcanal

My Dearest Helen,

I am on guard today 4 to 8 p.m. We haven't started training as we are still fixing up the camp. I am feeling fine, but getting tired of this kind of life and being away from home. I know it seems like a long time ago that I left. I hope you still love me when I come back.

On January 29th the Old Raiders (Rusty, Norm, Thor, R.D. McDowell and Spath), who had been in battle on Guadalcanal and Bougainville, got aboard ship to go back to the States. They said, "We are not coming back over here," that they would stay in the States and drive for a captain or colonel. They had two weeks leave (some of them took a bit longer). The Fifth Division was formed, and those that had the two-week leave started to train for Iwo Jima. They were sent to the big island of Hawaii at Hilo to train. Thor and Russell were killed on Iwo. Rusty, Norm and Spath were wounded after 12 or 13 days there.

Rusty said in his letter of February '85:

Ray with
gung-ho knives

Robert Lindsay on the beach at Guadalcanal.

I wonder if anyone ever got Russell to wear his helmet. He always said he couldn't hear anything with the damn thing on.

Russell was in the Makin raid celebration at Camp Allard that A & B companies had.

January 30th and 31st — We worked on our new camp. We were assigned our guns, and we put up tents, then trained until leaving.

I quit writing in my diary February 3rd, 1944.

February 3rd, I received a letter and valentine from Helen. I almost forgot about Valentine's Day.

Hi, Sweetie,

It is raining, and the surf is coming in rough. We have been moving again, as you can see I have a different address. I got a grass skirt from a native. It isn't very good, but I will try to send it to you.

I was disappointed I didn't get a picture for Christmas. Please send me a picture so I can get it before I leave this place.

It's cloudy so I am using a lantern. I had to clean the globe so I could see better. It gets tiresome just seeing a bunch of guys. I would like to get back and see some good old civilian people and other things instead of coconut trees, jungles and blue ocean.

I am in the 4th Marines now. My new address is on the envelope. Do you still work at Missouri Valley Stores? You are always in my heart.

February 11

My "love,"

We just got our show set up. Boy! It seems good to see a show again and hear some music. We saw the show, "The Watch on the Rhine." When it rains and we are at the show, we just sit out in it and get soaked and still enjoy the show, even if we do have to sit on coconut logs. They do get hard after a while.

February 20th, I received five letters dated January 21st through February 1st.

Dearest Helen,

I got two more shots in my arm yesterday. It's a little sore but will be okay in a few days. I just got in from swimming; it's good exercise. I need to get in shape again. I'm really gaining weight now, but I'll need it for reserve some day. I heard about you and Dotty getting stranded in Carrollton after finding a place to dance (jitterbug) and no one knew where you were. It would have been a long walk back to Marshall. I'm glad someone came along and gave you a ride. How are the rest of the "Belles"? I don't know Mary Ruth, but she sounds okay.

Helen, Dorothy (my sis), Mary Ruth Thomas and Hazel Leimkuler are good friends. Their nicknames are Terry, Dotty, Peachie and Cindy. They call themselves "The Four Belles." They had an apartment together for a while, and there is quite a story about how they tried to dress and cut up a chicken to cook.

When the old Raiders left, the rest of us were transferred to Regimental Weapons Company of the 4th Marines. We worked on our new camp and were assigned to 37MM guns. Tents were set up, and we trained for the next operation. I used to be a front line Marine; I am now an anti-tank man on a 37MM as assistant gunner.

Marine Raider units only existed from January 6, 1942 until February 1944.

Robert Lindsay transferred back to the Rifle Company, because he didn't get to be gun captain on the 37MM.

February 26th, I received letters dated January 24th and February 8th. I wrote:

37MM Tank Gun Crew. Left to right: Flager, Harrison, Taylor, Merrell, Garvey, Gils (gun captain).

My Sweetheart,

I just came in from the show area. They had five bouts of boxing. I really enjoyed it. I used to be a front-line Marine, but now I am an anti-tank man on the 37MM gun, and I like it.

How did you like having your fortune told and did the ouija board give you good answers? I bet it kept you guessing. Everyone writes and tells me how pretty you are.

Yes, darling, it's been many Saturday nights and many other days that we haven't been together, but we can make a full day of each one that I am home. It's too good to be true to think of getting home someday and to be with you.

My folks are always telling me how sweet you look and how nice you are. They make me want to see you just that much more.

Dearest Helen,

Ray Milland and three girls put on a show for us February 27th. The girls sang some songs that you had written were on the Hit Parade. I liked the song, "No Love, No Nothing," lots, too. I hope the words fit you; it was a good show.

It had been a long time since I had seen a white girl. The girls just made me homesick for you.

We went to the movies every night we could. When the old film would break, we would throw rocks at the projection shed. When the Army drove by and made noise on purpose so we couldn't hear, we were ready for them; we would rock their trucks as they went by.

March 1st I received four letters dated February 3rd, 9th, 10th and 16th. I wrote in code that we were leaving this place, destination unknown.

My Dear Helen,

I intended to write last night, but was too darn tired. I am feeling okay, so don't worry about me.

March 3

My Dearest Helen,

I received two letters dated February 12th and 14th.

Do you still stay in town with Mildred and Dotty? I guess you, Mary Ruth and Dotty and the rest of your girlfriends have a swell time together. Boy, do I miss those Saturday nights.

March 8

Dearest Helen,

Where was the Military Ball held? I bet you had a swell time. I sure hope you did because you deserve it. I would sure like a picture of you in your formal. Helen, I don't want you to miss out on a good time just because you think someone will tell me about it. It's nobody's business but yours. I won't get mad, but don't get the wrong idea that I want you to step out. I just want you to have a good time and be happy. Believe me, honey, please.

March 8th and 10th we were on maneuvers on the U.S.S. Warren. We were training.

I received two letters dated February 21st and 23rd.

Dearest Helen,

I'm glad Mary and June made it back okay. Mary was always so nice to me when I came out to see you.

I have the lantern lit, but the globe needs cleaning. Makes it a little hard to write.

March 14

My Sweetheart Helen,

I received the sweetest letter, film and gum the other night, but was unable to answer your letter then. Hope you are okay and happy. I'd give anything to be with you. (I told Helen in code that I would be unable to write for some time.)

One night we were at a show, sitting on coconut logs when it was announced on the loudspeaker to report back to camp and pack our sea bags.

U.S.S. Callaway to Emirau, 3-17-44 to 3-20-44

The next morning, March 17th, we boarded the U.S.S. Callaway. It took three days to go to Emirau. We landed and there were no Japs. They had left a few days before. We set up guns on the beach, as we had to stand watch for a counter attack. We were bombed at night by a stray Jap plane. It was a pretty and nice sandy beach. Our guns were under big trees — camouflaged.

Left: On the beach at Emirau, washing up.

Emirau was a small island where the U.S. wanted to build an airstrip, so the Seabees built one.

March 25th, I wrote a V-mail letter telling Helen it was the first day I could write, and told her in code that I was on Emirau. I practically live in the ocean; that's the only way to keep cool, and the sand feels good to my feet.

April 4th, the moon was shining bright, and it was misting rain, so there was a pretty rainbow at night.

On Emirau we used to swim out to the end of the coral reef, take a hand grenade, pull the pin and drop the hand grenade to the bottom of the ocean. It would stun the fish, and they would come to the top. Then we would have fish to eat.

We now call the Emirau operation "Bloody Emirau."

U.S.S. DuPage — To Guadalcanal, 4-12-44 to 4-15-44

We left Emirau on the U.S.S. DuPage April 12th and were back on Guadalcanal on the 15th.

Guadalcanal, 4-15-44 to 6-4-44

I sent Helen one dozen red roses for Easter.

We started training again. We were now in the First Provisional Marine Brigade, under the command of General Lemuel Shepherd, and began training for the attack on Guam.

"One dozen roses"   Guam had been seized December 10th,

Helen

1941, three days after Pearl Harbor. The old U.S. Marine barracks were at Sumay on the OROTE peninsula.

April 10

Dearest Helen,

I received five letters. They sure pepped me up. They were sure sweet. I've read them over and over again. I've been overseas about 13 months, so I'm on the downhill grade now. I hope to see you someday. I am okay and feeling fine.

April 15

My Dearest Helen,

I have received letters dated from February 24th to April 3rd, an Easter card, St. Patrick's card, and a Hello card with a red feather on it. I wish I could have written as often. (I told Helen by code that I was on Guadalcanal again.) Mail call was about like Christmas. I received so many letters from you and my folks. Also three packages of candy (good old chocolate candy, too).

I'm tired of this war, but I still like the Marines best.

The Marines are a small outfit, but they do a lot of fighting for its size. I am proud to be Marine. I try to act like one, too. I'm glad I'm fighting with the Marines. We are all about the same age, and we understand each other. Time is passing by, and that's what I like because I have just so long to stay over here; then I'll be home to see you. I washed clothes today; I scrubbed them with a brush.

April 17

Hello, Honey,

I sent you the roses because I love you. I would go crazy if it wasn't for you. You're always pepping me up with your sweet letters and the things you say. I'll be glad when that "tomorrow night" rolls around. That would be swell. I want you to go out and have a good time. I always trust you because I know you so well and we have talked to each other a lot. I know you can go out and have a swell time and still be a good girl.

April 20

We saw our first show in a month. I have been on six different ships and spent over two months aboard and traveled many a mile. The Marines stand guard and gun watch aboard ship. I don't like it aboard ships; it is too damn hot.

Back in Marshall, Mo., Helen says:

I got all dressed up in my brand new beautiful formal and went to a Military Ball at Missouri Valley College with an ROTC cadet. Just as we walked in the door, a photographer nabbed us, lined us up with some other couples and took our picture. My heart sank! I knew that picture would be in the *Marshall Democrat News,* and Ray would get the paper overseas. Even though Ray had told me to go out and have a good time, I knew this was not good! That picture ruined my entire evening and is still my biggest regret ever.

April 24

6¢ due on letter

Dearest Helen,

I guess you know I had a funny feeling run all the way through me when I saw your picture in the Marshall paper. Maybe I'm a little jealous and in love, too. I do realize we aren't going steady, but I do know I'm deeply in love with you. I hope you don't make a habit of just going with one certain guy. I'd rather see you go with them all. You know it doesn't take long to fall in love with someone, if you like him the least little bit.

I think we knew we loved each other the first night we were together. I'm not trying to tell you who to go with. I just hope we can get along when I get back; I believe we can. You're lots of fun, and I love you very much. Helen, you have the right to go with whom you want. I'm sure we can get along okay when I get back to you, honey. I'm not mad, just writing the way I feel.

You have probably heard about "Dear Friend" letters. About 60% of the boys who were engaged or deeply in love get these letters, telling them that she has gotten married.

Some people don't realize what we go through over here and think this war is a damn big picnic, but I sure don't. There are a lot of Soldiers, Sailors and Marines, too, that are having a good time. They are the ones that make it hard on us. Most of the boys are here because they have to be. I know that is my case. But now that I'm here, I want to do my part, and then I'm waiting for the day I get back to you and the others I love. We are helpless out here, so it's up to the girls however they want it. I'm feeling fine, so don't worry about me. I'll always love you. I'll write again soon.

April 27

My Dearest Helen,

I received four of the sweetest letters from you tonight. I didn't go to the show because I wanted to write to you. I don't enjoy shows out here any more. I think of home a lot and play cards to pass the time. The boys talk about their girlfriends and how nice they are. We play different kinds of sports and go to the movies some. Most of all, we write letters. We don't have much spare time, but we get by.

I like to show Helen's pictures and tell how nice she is and why I love her.

May 3

Dearest Darling,

I received the letter you wrote April 18th. Please send me a big picture. I haven't seen a recent picture of you. If I can't see you in person, I'll have to settle for a picture for a while. Please send me one, honey. I'm out here on this little island, and all I see is boys and more boys and coconut trees. I'd give anything in the world to see you and be with you, honey.

I'm on the downhill grade now, so you haven't so long to wait, but it is still quite a while. Time is passing for me. I hope it is for you. I really love you. I hope I dream of you, but I usually dream of Japs.

May 5

Dearest Helen,

I received two very sweet letters from you last night. They were written April 19th and 23rd. Thanks for the sweet picture. Honey, I hope you had a nice time at the prom — who is the lucky guy? I'd really like to be home so I could go with you. Helen, when you go out with some boy forget me and have a good time. There is nothing I hate worse than to go out with a girl and for her to talk about her boyfriend. I know you love me, and we'll have a swell time when I get back. You know for sure I love you. I'll be glad when you start getting my mail and I start getting your answers. I couldn't get along without your letters. A big kiss for Lizzie! Ha!

May 9

Dearest Darling,

What happened to Vesta and Eleanor? So Dotty is going to Kansas City to stay with my sis, Ernie. I wish I were home to take up some of your vacation time, that would be swell. I have a hard day ahead of me, so will close. Please keep writing to me often, and send me the picture I ask for.

May 12th to May 15th, we were on maneuvers on the U.S.S. Ormsby. Also May 23rd until leaving for Guam, we were training, landing and unloading ship. Climbing down the sides of ships with full pack, rifle, etc., getting into landing crafts and going ashore. We went back to Guadalcanal and trained until June 4th. We were training for the attack on Guam.

May 13th, I wrote Helen by code that I would be leaving this place, destination unknown, and that I would be unable to write for some time.

May 18

Dearest Helen,

I received three letters from you four or five days ago, but have been so busy I haven't written to anyone. When I got in tonight, I was dirty and plenty tired, but I received several letters from home and from you, dear. I received the letters from you dated April 24th and 25th, and the eight-page book dated May 3rd. Thanks for the prayers, I'll need lots of them. It makes me happy to know I'm in your heart. I would have loved to be with you in the park listening to the water run over the rocks.

Now I'll try to answer your eight-page letter. Helen, I really enjoyed the letter very much, even if you did tell me off a little. It makes me love you more to know you have a little "spunk," or temper. Helen, I didn't care for you going with Jim. I just told you I had a funny feeling when I saw your picture. I can't help it if I love you, can I? Helen, I know what kind of girl you are; that's why I love you. You took that letter wrong, I'm sure. Honey, if I didn't trust you, I would never have loved you like I do, please believe me.

Helen, you wrote a very sensible letter and stated a lot of true facts. I don't care what you do when you go out with someone. I don't want to know of your love affairs, just so you know I still love you. Tear up that letter and forget all about it. You have received other letters since then. I'm sorry I hurt your feelings. I feel like crying when I read your letters. I know how you feel, but you got me wrong. Sometimes I get the blues so bad I don't care if I live or die. This war is hell on everyone.

May 20

Hi, Honey,

I received the sweet letters from you tonight dated May 12th. Boy, was I glad to hear from you again. Thanks for the picture, but I'm still waiting for the big one. It's summer time and I still want one of you in a bathing suit. I received a letter from Elsie Matheny; she really said some nice things about you. It makes me proud of you. She and her family sent me cookies and candy for Christmas. I hope you get to work at the telephone company this summer. Hope the old school bus doesn't break down any more.

May 22

My Dearest Helen,

I received two sweet letters from you dated May 4th and 10th. Sweetheart, you must have been in Iceland when you wrote the letter on the 4th. Helen, if I didn't love you, that picture wouldn't have affected me the way it did. You must have dreamed about that letter all night and then got mad. Are you still mad? If you are, I can't do anything about it. I hope you still love me as much as ever, and forget that damn letter. Thanks for the clover. I probably will need it the way things look.

May 28

Hello, Darling,

I received two of the sweetest letters from you yesterday, dated May 11th and 14th. Boy, they sure pepped me up. I'm glad you're okay and still think of me once in a while. I had to hunt up a can so I could get some kerosene to fill the lantern so I could write to you. That was a cute letter with the pansy in it. It still had its color and smell. I'm saving it.

We don't get much fresh food or meat (everything is dehydrated), just enough to keep us going. Some good fresh eggs and green vegetables — I sure could tear into them.

Do you remember the night when your dad, you and I played cards? Those were the good old days. I'm always thinking of you and the good times we had together.

I saw in the paper about Joe and Elsie's baby. How is he getting along? How are Roger and Joyce? I'm glad Edward got to come home.

U.S.S. Ormsby, 6-4-44 to 7-21-44, 47 days

June 4th, we boarded the U.S.S. Ormsby for the invasion of Guam. The landing was planned to take place three days after the attack on Saipan, on June 15th. The problems on Saipan caused a postponement of our landing on Guam. We remained afloat as a mobile reserve.

We would sail away from Guam and Saipan at night and in the daytime sail toward them. The Japs were putting up such a battle on Saipan we thought we would have to go there. We were about 100 miles off Saipan.

June 9

My Dearest Helen,

I'm sure glad the invasion of Europe came off okay. It makes the war look better. I'm going into combat again. I'll make it okay, so don't worry. You'll probably know where I am by the time you receive this. Be sure to keep writing. I'll write every chance I get. You know I love you.

Remember the night you went to the football game with your girlfriends? You were mad at me, but later I saw you and got to take you home to Mary's apartment. However, I wouldn't let you go in until you said I could see you the next night.

I have three pictures of you with me. They have been everywhere with me out here, so you are really seeing the world. My pictures are turning yellow from setting in the wet foxholes on Bougainville.

I told Helen by code that I was going to Guam. My sis Dotty is working in Kansas City this summer and staying with my sister Ernie. Helen is staying in Marshall with her sister Mary and is working at the Cut Price Clothing Store as assistant bookkeeper. Cut Price Store is a men's shoe and clothing store.

June 13

My Dearest Helen,

I hate writing on this damn Navy stationery! I received six letters from you. Boy, was I glad to get them; they really helped me out. I read them over and over. You are doing your part, keeping my morale up.

This letter will be late getting to you. I won't be able to write for some time, but please be sure to keep writing to me. Your letters help me so much. I'm glad you liked the shells and painting I sent.

Well, I have two brothers in the Navy now, so I'm the lone Marine, but I'm glad I'm a Marine. A Marine is a soldier of the sea.

I'm glad you like your new job at the Cut Price Store.

July 1st I wrote a V-mail letter:

My Dearest Helen,

Somewhere in the Pacific, I'm still okay, but have been unable to write. It's been some time since I heard from you, but I know it isn't your fault. I'll be glad when I can write often again and can get your letters. I still think of you every day, and I'd sure like to be sitting out on the front porch with you. We would stay there until everyone else went inside, wouldn't we? You know I won't stand you up on that "tomorrow night" date.

Robert Lindsay told me to write you to thank you for writing to his aunt. Helen, tell my mother I'm okay. I might not get to write to her right now, but I'll do my best. Remember, I'll always love you. I'll be glad when I can write to you often again and get your sweet letters. Write often.

July 7th, I received over 30 letters, half of them from Helen. They sure helped me out.

My Dearest Helen,

I'm really in a happy mood. I hope I'm home to go to the prom with you next year; that would be the dream of my life. I'll probably be home before then, but I don't know when. I received a letter from Dorothy; she said she missed you more than she missed Mom and Dad. So do I, honey. I love you with all my heart.

I should get some more mail in a few days. I wish I could have written you as many letters as I have received, but I just couldn't write.

July 10th they dumped us off on a small island (Coral Atoll) close to Eniwetok in the Marshall Islands for one day to air out the ship and for us to stretch our legs. It was hot and no shade. We had C rations to eat, and we were there only one day.

July 12

My Dearest Helen,

I have been overseas 16 months today; that's a long time to be away from you. My mom said she saw your picture at Gilkeys. Are you sending me a big one? I sure hope so.

July 14

My Sweetheart,

How about me getting you a nice cedar chest for Christmas? I've been thinking about asking you for a long time, now that you have your own apartment. I've been thinking of you and wishing we were together.

Our landing on Guam was on July 21st. We had been on the ship 47 days.

MESSAGE BEFORE GUAM INVASION

Marines from the First Provisional Marine Brigade, commanded by Brigadier General Lemuel C. Shepherd, landed here fully aware that they had "a personal score to settle" with the Japanese.

Just before the Marines landed, Brig. Gen. Shepherd, in a message to his officers and men, said:

"Your commanding General desires to wish all hands God-speed in the approaching operation.

"As you are all aware, this brigade has been given the honor of participating in the recapture of United States territory — ground on which Marines were stationed for 40 years until overcome by superior enemy forces. Our corps has a personal score to settle in the landing we are about to effect.

"This will be our first operation as a brigade. Our regiments have demonstrate their combat efficiency in previous battles. We must now fight together as a team. I have every confidence in your ability to accomplish our mission. United States Marines never fail. Good luck to each of you, and may God protect us in all dangers."

Guam, 7-21-44 to 8-28-44

We were all scared. They took us in on landing crafts as far as possible. They hit coral reefs that the boats could not get over. So we got out in waist-high water and pulled 37MM guns, mounted on two wheels, ashore. We were shelled and shot at. A lot of men were killed on the beach. We got ashore and pushed in about 100 to 150 yards the first day and dug in. We dug a hole for our gun and one for our foxhole. During the night the Japs counter-attacked.

We were lucky to be in the right spot at the right time. The next day we extended the beach head. My foxhole was right on the beach. The ships were shooting illumination shells (star shells) to light up the beach area. We were there two nights. One time a star shell lit up just as a dog was running down the beach. We thought it was a Jap, but we noticed in time that it was a dog and no one fired.

The sand fleas were very bad. I would tell Garvey I was going to take a nap in the foxhole, but the fleas bit me so bad I would tell him to catch some shut-eye while I stood watch. Later I would try again to get some sleep, without any success.

We were relieved on the front line, then took position to advance toward the Oroto Peninsula where the air field and old Marine barracks were before the war.

July 28th, the first night out, I took deathly sick and was put in the field hospital.

They had quite a battle on the Oroto Peninsula that night. Robert Lindsay was in the thick of the battle.

The first night in the hospital we had heavy rain, and the water got up to the canvas on the cots. Everything was floating. The next morning we were evacuated and moved to higher ground. I was very ill with dysentery and a high fever and so weak I couldn't get out of bed. I was in the hospital four or five days; then I told them I had to get out so I could get well. I talked the doctor into releasing me, and I had to hitchhike all the way across the island to my outfit.

July 30th while in the hospital I wrote:

My Dearest Helen,

I guess you know by now that I am participating in the action on Guam. I'm feeling as good as could be expected. I'm pretty well worn out and tired. I'm getting a little rest now; I'll feel tops in a day or two. At last we are fighting on American soil. Guam is not like the rest of the islands. It is more civilized and not as many jungles. Excuse this short letter. I've got to get some rest.

I got a ride in a truck and was almost back to my outfit the first night, but had to stay with an artillery company. I ate supper with them; we had navy beans and corn bread, and it tasted good.

I got up at 4 a.m. the next morning and left with the artillery company and found my outfit about 7 a.m., just as they were going back to the front lines.

My company had camped at a Jap beer dump and had their trucks loaded with Jap beer and Saki in all the empty spaces.

By being in the 37MM anti-tank gun crew, we didn't go to the front lines until night. So the guys drank beer all day in a little old building; the floor was covered with rice. They drank and sang. I couldn't handle any of that, just getting out of the hospital, still weak and with an upset stomach.

That night we set up in a circle of defense. Everything in front was enemy territory. I was on guard at 1 a.m. (I was the only one awake after the others had been drinking all day), when three Japs came walking down the road next to some brush. I threw a clod over to Joe Harrison who was on the machine gun. He started firing; then everyone else started firing. The three Japs were killed.

The next morning before sun-up, some of the guys were out searching the dead Japs for souvenirs. One of the Japs was a doctor, and two were riflemen. All carried rifles.

The fighting continued until Guam was secured. Guam was worse than Bougainville. There were not as many jungles, and there were still snipers in caves.

I was very tired and had worn my clothes a month without washing. The flies were really bad, and they bothered me a lot.

The Guamanian people are glad we're back. I don't know if I'm glad we're back or not, but it isn't such a bad island.

August 17

Hello, Honey,

Gee, it seems swell to be able to write to you again. I have received several lettes from you that I haven't answered. Guam is secured now, so I'm getting some rest. I washed my clothes yesterday; they were pretty dirty, and so was I. I had worn my clothes a month without washing them.

I'm feeling pretty good now and will feel better when I get a few more days rest. We were kept on the go. You can tell by this writing that I'm a little stirred up.

You make me hungry talking about ice cream suppers. I could eat five gallons right now.

I saw Robert Lindsay for the first time in three months. He made it okay, too. I will see him quite a bit now. He said he heard from you.

The fleas are really bad here, and they bother me.

August 24

My Darling,

It's been sometime since I got a letter from you. I guess you are taking your vacation. Did you go to Kansas City? It's about time for school to start again, and I'm still out here in this Godforsaken country, but I'll be home someday. Stand by for "tomorrow night."

I washed my clothes again this morning, so I'm a clean lad again.

The native people here on Guam speak English pretty well; it seems funny to be able to talk to them. The natives tell us all about the Japs that were here. They sure pulled some dirty tricks. There are still quite a few snipers left in caves, but we'll get rid of them someday. I wish I could tell you more about what I went through and my experiences since I have been out here, but it will have to wait until I get back.

After Guam was about secured, three of us went out and found a cave and a five-inch gun. There was a bunch of gun explosives shaped like spaghetti in a five-inch round that would make the gunfire. We got the spaghetti-looking explosive and made a pile inside the cave. We sprinkled the spaghetti and string out of the cave and lit it. When it got to the big pile inside the cave, it exploded. No Japs came out.

Guam Liberators — 1st Prov. M Brigade U.S. ATS Pennat, 8-28-44 to 9-8-44

We got aboard the U.S. ATS Pennat on August 28th. The first night out a lot of us slept topside in the cool. The next morning the shoes of Milton Bankhead from Oakland, California were found. They had roll call and he didn't show up. The ship radioed back to Guam for a search plane. He was spotted and picked up the next day. He had fallen over with his life jacket on and had been in the water about 20 hours. His eyes were sunburned, and he was water-soaked. He was in the hospital four to six weeks. He returned to our company and was in on the invasion of Okinawa with us.

On the ship I thought of home constantly; I sure got lonesome. It sounded good when Helen told me in her letters about feeding the chickens and walking around the farm. It was impossible to write on the ship. We slept topside because of the heat. We took salt water showers, but we did get enough fresh water to brush our teeth and shave. In the daytime we played cards to pass time.

I now have three stars in my campaign ribbon.

September 4th, orders were received from the Commandant of the Marine Corps directing that the First Provisional Marine Brigade be redesignated as the Sixth Marine Division.

Guadalcanal, 9-8-44 to 3-12-45

September 8th we arrived at Guadalcanal, and we started training to go to Okinawa.

September 11

Hi, Honey Bunch,

It has been three weeks since I have been able to write to any-one. I have a good excuse, but it's against censorship to explain it, so you'll just have to excuse me again. I have received many letters from you. It is swell of you to write, and to know you still love me. I have received many packages from home, but the best gift was the large picture you sent me. Thanks a million; I treasure it above all. (I told Helen by code that I was back on Guadalcanal.)

I was always thinking of you and wishing we were together even though I couldn't write.

Robert Lindsay and I are still in the same outfit, but in differ-ent companies. I get to see him lots now. He was on Guam, but we were on different ships; that was the reason we didn't see one an-other. Remember when I used to tell you when we went on different hikes when we were on New Caledonia? We still go on hikes, but it's news now, so I don't mention it any more.

I'll tell you a little about life aboard a transport ship. I've been on eight different ships and spent over 125 days aboard. It is usu-ally crowded and hot. We have good chow, but it's so hot in the mess hall you can't enjoy it, and it's so hot in the holes where we sleep that we usually sleep topside where it is cool. I don't mind the ship too much, but I'm glad I'm not a sailor.

You ask about the girl I have been writing to. I should have told you about it, I know, but it is nothing. She has been writing to me about a year, and this year not over 15 letters. I can truthfully say I haven't written over eight letters, so you can see it is nothing seri-ous, so think nothing of it, please. I hope you forgive me. Remember you didn't tell me you were going with Jim. At least, I haven't had my picture in the paper with her. Let's forget this "crap." I love you and you love me, don't you, honey?

The song "I'll Be Seeing You" must be pretty; it sure has a good title. I know I would sure love to see you. Now how about a long letter from you?

September 16

My Darling Helen,

I have been thinking of you day and night, but just put off writing because of the inconvenience we have out here — no lights and other things. I was looking for a letter from you tonight, but I didn't get one.

When I was aboard ship this last time, I thought of you and being home constantly. Gee, it would be heaven to be with you again. I still think of you as being my wife some day.

September 20

Dearest Helen,

I received the sweet letter you wrote to me dated September 10th. It sure helped me out. I'm so lonely for you. You know I wouldn't neglect you to write to Carrollton; you know I love you more than that. When I'm aboard ship, it's impossible to write; it isn't my fault that you don't hear from me often. I'm always thinking of you even though I don't get to write. I'm having no picnic. I'd sure love to hear from you more often now, honey. The longer I'm over here, the more I miss you.

How are you and Jim getting along now? You know that song, "Please Leave My Girl Alone"? I'm helpless out here, but I trust you with all my heart, so I won't worry about Jim. You know I still love to tease my honey. No!

Robert Lindsay came by, and we walked over to the show. It was "What a Woman"; it was just fair. The boys out here are wolfish when they see a love scene. Everyone yells, "Kiss her," and so on. It will seem swell to be able to see a show in peace again, and lots better if you are sitting beside me. No news — we just sit around and talk of home and the ones we love.

Robert Lindsay

Ray taking a swim

I still wanted to get into something to get off the front line, so I checked with "Frenchie," the mess sergeant. He said he would give me a try, but another guy was to try out first; his name is "Fireball" Schultz.

Frenchie the mess sergeant.

We have a Marine Band now. It's pretty good and gives us some good entertainment.

We have been busy fixing camp, laying cement for a building. It's 8:30, and I just got off work. I was using a wheelbarrow, and we used truck lights to see to work. I have some kind of rash on my shoulder from cutting logs, but it isn't bad.

September 26

Hello, Sweetheart,

I received two letters from you last night. They sure made me happy. I'm feeling tops and still thinking of you every day. I'm very lonely for you.

Sweetheart, wouldn't it be swell to sit out on a blanket under a nice shade tree with each other and just forget about the war and talk things over? Gee, that would be heaven for me. Please keep trying to get film for me. I know it's hard to get, but it's worth a lot to me.

I get so tired seeing coconut trees. I'd give anything to sit under a good old elm or maple tree; that's all I think of lately. I get so lonesome. I could sure go for some good fried chicken and ice cream. Everyone seems to be in the "dumps" out here. We would all like to go home, but I guess everyone feels that way once in a while. I like the song, "I'll Walk Alone," but "I'll Be Seeing You" fits me better.

Marine Band

We have been training hard, and I don't have much time to write.

The moon is pretty over the ocean, and it leaves a streak of light on the water. It makes me homesick. I dream of sitting on a soft sofa, listening to pretty music on the radio, and forgetting about the war, having good things to eat, seeing civilized people and pretty girls, being under a shade tree, or having a good snowball fight, a sleigh ride or ice skating, seeing a good movie in a good comfortable seat and being able to hear it, but mostly about being with you. I don't enjoy a show out here any more. We can't hear it, and the sound makes it worse.

My morale is getting low; being away from home for two years is too darn long for me. I didn't have any idea it would be this long. I'd give anything to see everyone.

Robert Lindsay and I go to church services together on Sundays and play horseshoes.

They keep us pretty busy so we can't think of home too much.

We've been able to get gum and candy at the PX lately. I guess we get enough to get by.

September 30

My Darling Helen,

I washed a lot of clothes and cleaned my rifle. We really have a tough training schedule this time, but it will get a guy in shape to do his job. It won't be too long until we can be together. I don't know when, but I have a good feeling lately.

October 7

Dearest Darling,

I received your two very nice letters of September 25th and 27th. Your letters always make a different person out of me, because I'm so happy then. I get so lonesome for you, I get down in the dumps at times.

I see Robert a good bit now; we talk about what we are going to do when we get back. Please keep writing often and send me pictures.

October 10

My Darling Helen,

It seems ages ago since I had a letter from you; it hasn't been too long, but it seems long because I love to get your letters. I know you could write more letters than you do. I guess you're tired of writing to me.

Do you remember when we used to leave your house and just as soon as we got on the road I'd hold your hand and you always gave me a big smile? How about another picture for Christmas? I'd sure love to have one. Now be good and write me a nice long letter.

October 15

My Darling,

It sure pepped me up when I got in tonight and I had a sweet letter from you, dated October 1st.

The mosquitoes aren't so bad here now. We have no grass in our camp and the wind blows a lot. They don't like the wind, so they stay in the swamps. We sleep under mosquito nets at night anyway.

Time is passing pretty fast for me now because they are keeping us busy. I still like to swim, but I don't go much any more.

October 23

My Dearest Helen,

I received three letters from you tonight; one letter was dated June 30. I guess it got on the wrong truck, but it was still swell to get it. You were telling me about the beauty contest you were in at the Auditorium Theater. I wish I could have been the judge.

October 29

My Darling Helen,

It's cool here now and the sun is shining through out tent. The ocean is calm, and it looks like a sheet of glass with the sun shining on it. I received your letters of October 16th and 18th.

I'm going to church with Robert in a little while. I'm going down to his company to church, then he is coming up to our company for noon chow. Red is sure a good-hearted, swell guy.

November 1

Darling Helen,

It's been a few days since I heard from you, but it seems like weeks. A year ago we made the beachhead on Bougainville. It was my first action against the Japs. I stood watch the night before, looking for Jap planes.

Did you get to Kansas City to see Harry James? If so, did you have a good time?

How tall are you now, and how much do you weigh? I love you so much. Are you getting tired of waiting for me? I know you are, but we'll get together again, fairly soon. I'm sure tired being away from you. I miss you a lot.

November 5

My Darling Helen,

I received three letters from you; they were swell, they seemed so much like you. I'm so happy our hearts are still very close; that helps me a lot.

I'm glad you got to see Harry James. I know he was good. I would have loved to be with you, too, darling. I love you so much, and was always so happy when we were together. I have two years of my love saved up for you and the love for the rest of my life is yours. My life depends on you, honey, everything you do is part of me — your happiness — your love — your troubles — everything, darling. I hope this letter has the same effect on you as it has on me. You seem to be here with me, making me happy. I believe I'm closer to you now than I've been for a long time. Gosh, what a good feeling!

I think it's your sweet letters that make me feel so good now. I know you could make me happy the rest of my life.

I don't care what you do when school is out. The Cadet Nurse Corps is okay, but darling, I want to be with you all the time when I get home. I don't want you to be tied down to something. Think it over, get a good job there in town. You should be able to stand the grind in Marshall if I can stand it over here. I'm waiting for you always. Go out and have a good time; we can start in where we left off when I get back.

November 8

My Darling Helen,

I received your letter of October 28th, also the fruit cake and things you sent. They were in excellent condition. Thanks a lot for the film and other things.

A year ago tonight was the worst night of my life. I was on Bougainville. It rained all night, the water was knee deep in our foxholes and, of course, the Japs were causing us trouble, too.

It has started to rain here now. It's the rainy season, so it will be a little cooler for a few months.

November 12

My Darling,

The Marine Corps birthday was the 10th of this month. We had a U.S.O. show. No girls, just men entertaining us. We still get to see shows, but I don't seem to enjoy them.

I'm glad you like your work. I know you have a good boss.

November 15

Dearest Darling Helen,

Helen, you're swell, you are getting in the groove, writing to me like you used to. I received two more very sweet letters. I'm so happy when I hear from you. I remember how you used to smile at me, and my heart would just beat all the faster.

Robert was up to go to the show, but I wanted to write letters. The show was Ann Miller in "Jam Session." A show like that makes me homesick for you.

I'm glad you received the Marine Corps Chevron and enjoyed it. By reading it, you might learn some Marine slang.

November 17

Dearest Helen,

We had a U.S.O. show; Bob Crosby put it on. No girls. It was the best show I have seen out here. Most of them are no good.

November 20

My Darling Helen,

I have been awfully busy, but not too busy to think of you. I received a very sweet letter from you last night and another Christmas package. It was in very good condition and everything fixed up so pretty. I know you spent a lot of time with it. Thanks a million for everything.

I got a big kick out of the "Spam" you sent. Now don't feel bad, but that's the kind of meat we eat all the time out here, and we get plenty tired of it. Have you ever seen in the "Leatherneck" magazine or the "Chevron" jokes about Spam? Everyone out here gets a big laugh when they see a Spam page in a magazine. They make it look so good; you know what I mean.

I know I won't be over here many more months. I guess Paul and Nelson will get home for Christmas or before. We'll be together someday, and I'm just waiting for that day.

Thank you for the figs and dates. You're doing swell sending me film. You are sure to get some pictures ASAP. Thank you for the 1945 calendar. I hope I don't have to use it out here, and I'm sure I won't have to use it back home to make my dates with you, because I want to be with you every minute I can.

I pinned up some more of your pictures today. I told you once that you are my pin-up girl. How about some more pictures?

Thanksgiving Day, 1944

My Dearest Helen,

I have been away from home and missed three Thanksgiving days, but I enjoyed this one better than the others. We had a fair dinner today, but I long for some good home cooking. The first Thanksgiving I was in St. Louis. I had just left you and missed you so much. The last one I was on Bougainville.

I received two letters from you and a birthday card from you and one from Mary.

So Jimmy is back already. I hate to bitch, but he left the States after I did. He doesn't deserve to be back. He has probably never been shot at. I don't blame him, but we're all human out here. The Marines are doing lots of fighting and not getting anything for it, just because we are a small outfit and can't get replacements. I could talk all night about the way they do things; it really makes me mad.

Robert's brother came out about a month before we did, and he went back in May or June. The boys deserve it if they just come over, if they would just ship the oldest back first.

I get to feeling that way quite often. I need you to help me forget these years that we have been apart. I know we'll be the happiest couple in the world.

I saw in the paper where you were captain of a softball team. Do you really like basketball? How many points do you make in a game?

December 1

My Darling,

We have two or three boats here on the beach, and some of the boys go out in them. They have to paddle them, so they don't go far. They have fun diving off them. They would probably try to paddle back to the U.S.A. if they thought they could make it. So would I. I'd do most anything to be with you.

I received lots of Christmas packages. I can hardly wait to open the letter of yours.

December 4

My Dearest Helen,

I know I won't be over here many more months. We have stood it two years. I know we can wait a few more months, can't we?

Mom sent me the pictures they took when Ned was home. I treasure them because you are in them. You look swell.

I read in the papers where all the country schools are having box suppers. I wish I was there to go with you. I remember the one at Antioch School. I think your dad was bidding against me for the box you fixed!

December 11

My Darling Helen,

Here it is my birthday. I had a swell birthday because I received two letters from you. They make me so happy.

I don't enjoy a show any more. All I care about is getting your letters and pictures. All I think about is you and home. You are my "Post War Plan." How do you like that?

I wish you had accepted the cedar chest for Christmas.

December 15

My Darling Helen,

I received the Christmas card from your sis Mil, and the nice letter in it. I sure enjoyed it. Her letter was so nice and thoughtful. I can never express what it means to me.

I also received a swell letter and Christmas card from your mother. You can't realize what a letter from her meant to me. I'd sure love to see your folks, they were always so swell to me. I know you miss Mary. I know she is a swell sister to you. So you are keeping the apartment, why don't you stay with Mil and Dotty?

I'm getting serious. I'd love to marry you. I know we could make it. What do you say we get engaged when I get home and we get along okay? I don't want to get married until this war is over, so we won't have to part again. Do you ever think you would like to marry me?

I sure hope I get home by the time school is out. Helen, please don't tie yourself down to something so we can't be together, be-

*cause all I'm living for now is you and our happiness together. With-
out you to love and write to, I would go crazy over here, but I still
know there is one sweet girl in the U.S.A. who still loves me, and
my life depends on; that's you, darling.*

December 17

My Darling Helen,

*Now don't fall over, but I'm going to be a cook and cook for 200
men in our company. "Fireball" Schultz didn't work out as a cook,
so now I get my chance. I am now assistant cook, and I made Corporal. I've got a chance to get ahead, and that's what counts out
here. I've done my part on the front line fighting face to face with
the Japs. I'll still be doing my share. I'll still have to fight until we
secure a beachhead, but I know how when the time comes. I get
tired of training the same thing over and over again. All I want is
to be with you and settle down. That would be heaven for me.*

My sis, Mildred, got Helen a gold compact, housecoat and house
slippers for me for Christmas. I received lots of letters, cards and
gifts from home, cards and letters from her mother, Mary and
Mildred. They all meant a lot to me.

December 25

Darling Helen,

*I opened the letter that had the ID bracelet in it. It's pretty and
very nice, and I sure treasure it. I enjoyed the card also.*

*I worked all day cooking a Christmas dinner for 200 men. It
was so hot here everyone went without shirts and just wore shorts.
I made another rate, Sergeant and Field Cook.*

*We had turkey and everything. It was good for out here. Robert
came up and ate dinner with our company.*

*We had coconut branches and buried lots of them for a Christ-
mas tree. We had red light bulbs on them at the Regimental Chapel.
It sure didn't look like the old pine trees at home, but we tried to get
the Christmas spirit.*

*We got four bottles of beer today; we don't get much. I don't like
it anyway. We got 12 Cokes the other day, the most I've gotten since
I've been overseas. It sure tasted good, too. Can you get Cokes at
home? Your letters were dated December 8th, 9th and 11th. Keep
your letters flying. I love them all.*

It won't be long until New Year's will be around, and I'm still out here waiting for the day we can be together and be happy again, and always.

I got five more shots in the arm today.

December 28

My Darling Helen,

I'm feeling fine, but lonesome for you. It's been raining all day and still is. Well, anyway it's cool for a change. I received two letters yesterday dated December 3rd and 18th, but didn't have time to answer. You ask me what the barrels were for. They are for water and trash. Those are lister bags that we get our drinking water from; we have trucks to fill them. Those pictures were taken when we just got back from Guam and I had lost some weight, but have gained it back now.

I'm always thinking of things I'd like to do, and you're always with me. I'd love to be married to you, but I get to thinking I couldn't do enough for you.

There is a U.S.O. show tonight with girls in it. I guess it's fairly good, but they just lower my morale, and I wanted to write to you, so didn't go. I know I love you too much. I want to make you happy so bad, I don't know what to do. I'd like to talk to you about a lot of things. We can be happy together, I know. I received a Christmas card from Mary. It's swell of her to think of me, and it means a lot to me. I can remember when she would be there when I used to come out for you. She was always so cheerful, just like you.

I remember when I used to throw Roger up in the air and he would want me to keep it up. He would say, "Do it again."

No, I haven't received the Life Magazine. I'm sending another picture of me and a friend of Robert Lindsay.

New Year's night

My Darling Helen,

I was getting ready to hit the hay, but I stepped out of the tent and went to the beach. Well anyway, the ocean was so pretty and it made me wish I were with you.

Everyone seems to be up waiting for the New Year, the ones who are feeling good anyway. I don't believe I will stay up. I'm fairly tired tonight, but I'm always thinking of you, no matter how tired I am or what I'm doing. I have lots of letters to write, but you are always first.

I received the nice letter you wrote the night you opened the Christmas presents I got for you. I'd sure have loved to give them to you in person.

I guess you get to see Mary lots even though she is in Kansas City. I hope I'm home before you go somewhere to get a job. I received a nice letter from Mil and Ray, Dot and my folks. Gosh, it's nice to hear from home, and I couldn't make it if it weren't for your letters and love.

January 10

My Darling Helen,

As you could see, I didn't get to finish my letter I started to you January 4th. I've been busy. We just got in from a field problem. It's really hot here today as always. I think I'll take a swim in the ocean to cool off. I wish I were with you. I'd even settle for a snowball fight. I'll do my best to write to you as often as I can now, while it's possible. To be with you and plan the future is all I think of. I love you.

January 12

My Darling Helen,

We had a big mail call last night, and I received five of the sweetest letters from you. Boy! They were swell, and just like you. I wish I could write to you as often.

I'm just putting in my time, hoping to get back to you ASAP. I'm planning on having a swell time with you when I get back. I hope we can get enough gas to go places and do things. Are you ready to go?

So you are a bowler now! That's a lot of fun. Where is the bowling alley?

I guess I'm getting along okay as a cook. It's really hard work. I get up at 3:30 in the morning and work late at night, according to the fresh meat we have to cut up. We don't get fresh meat often, but we sure enjoy it when we do. I'll learn how to butcher a little. It's hot to work over the hot stove. We have field stoves, and they use gas.

I don't eat very regular now. I don't believe I feel as good as I did when I was a rifleman. Cooking has its advantages and disadvantages, too. I'll still go into action. We won't start cooking until the place has quieted down a bit.

Just as soon as you said Mary was going to Kansas City to work, I knew you would go sooner or later. I sure hope to get home by the time school is out.

While on Guadalcanal, I would make an eight-gallon pot of pudding, using one pound of corn starch, ten pounds of sugar, one pound of cocoa, and 24 cans of canned milk. I burned my stomach frying eggplant with no shirt on. Our stoves were always breaking down, and we would have to work on them. We looked more like mechanics than cooks.

We were getting in some beef from Australia in burlap sacks, partially frozen, in a portable cooler. They were leaking . We cut steaks out of it, had stew and Swiss steak. Smitty, the mess sergeant (head cook), would invite us in after we were through cooking to eat filet mignon that he had cooked.

Robert Lindsay and Joe Hiott from his rifle company would come up to our mess hall when I was on duty to eat. They said the food was better than in their company.

Smitty, head cook

We were sent ice cream mix, but we had no way of freezing it, so we would mix it up and drink it.

When we were aboard ship, we boiled cold storage eggs in a big steam kettle; they smelled funny.

I got five more shots in my arm.

January 16

My Helen,

I received five letters from you. You'll never know how much I treasure your letters. They mean everything to me. You make me so happy. I love you so much, and I trust you. I have been out here so long, it seems like a dream to have a girl like you to love me so much, but I know it's more than a dream, because we loved each other when we had to part.

I was at work last night when I got your swell letters. Robert Lindsay was up, and he told me I had a letter from you, so I went to

my tent, and there was a letter from you, darling. Then another boy told me I had some more letters from you, so I looked in my box, and there was a letter on each side of your picture and two in my box. I looked at your picture, and it seemed as though you were smiling at me. I smiled back. Gosh! I had a good feeling.

I'm sitting here in our mess hall writing to you. It's cooler than in my tent. It's just 20 yards from here to the ocean. I can hear the waves on the beach. The water is really blue and not a ship in sight.

You were telling me about your locket. I let Robert Lindsay read that part of your letter. He said you were "snowing" me, telling me about showing my picture and the girls falling for me. He said he couldn't see what you saw in me. I told him that we all couldn't be good-looking.

Helen, I really don't care for any other girl. Sometimes I think that I want to see Lora Lee. I don't hear from her much any more. I guess she's found another guy. I never did love her; she's just not the kind for me.

January 18

My Darling Helen,

I received three sweet letters from you again tonight. I was thinking of you all day as usual and planning on writing to you. I also heard from Dad and Ned.

The moon isn't full, but it is a quarter. There are a few stars out around the moon. It's pretty to look through the coconut trees at the moon; it's just like a picture.

I enjoy your letters, so keep them flying.

You can ask all the questions you want when I get back, but most of all, I want to forget about the war and you can help me. We can plan our future together, have lots of fun, laugh and have good times.

I received a letter from Ned. He said not to plan on having too big a time when I get back, because there is nothing to do, but that's the least of my worries. Just to be with you, I'll be the happiest person on earth. I can sit in a soft chair, listen to the radio with you and be so happy. I'll appreciate the least little thing — a soft bed, the green grass; to be alone with you will be heaven.

Ned said there were a lot of girls in Marshall, but there is only one I want, and that is you, Helen. I mean that with all my heart. I'm kinda afraid you might run across some guy you like better. I know it sounds bad to you, but it has happened. I know it will break my heart if it does, but I trust you. You have waited two years for me. I know it's hard to do.

January 26

My Dearest Helen,

It's been several days since I wrote to you. We have been in the field a few days, so was unable to write. I received three very sweet letters from you tonight. I've really missed being where I could write, but have been thinking of you. Robert is up, so we are writing letters. We got some Coke again, I was surprised. We pay eight cents a bottle, but it's rationed to us so we don't get it often.

It has been nearly three years since we started going together, seven months of real fun together and the rest wishing we were together, receiving each other's letters to make us both happy.

January 28

My Sweetheart Helen,

I received your very sweet letter of the 16th tonight. Robert has been up most of the day. He's been reading some book. He is just like a kid even if he is 28. All we talk about is getting home. He wants you and me to come to St. Louis to visit.

I received a letter from my sis, Mil. She said she found a cedar chest for you that I asked her to get for me for your birthday. I hope you received it on your birthday and hope you like it.

It is now 8:45 p.m. It just started raining, and I just finished cutting meat for hamburgers for tomorrow's dinner. We don't get much fresh meat, so we sure enjoy it when we do.

What do you think about me cooking now? I know I have done my part on the front line fighting. I'm just doing a regular job now. It's a lot harder work, but I don't mind it. It makes the time pass quicker for me. I'll be in just as much danger when we hit the beach, but when we get a beachhead it will be a bit safer. No matter where you are, you can still get hurt. For instance, when we got back from Bougainville the first night, everyone thought we would get a good night's sleep. Well, it started to rain, and the wind started blowing hard. A coconut tree fell and killed a boy that everyone knew, but that is war. You can never plan anything.

Please send me a snapshot picture of you. I can hardly wait 'til I can be with you but there is nothing to do but wait. I've really been true to you, but it's not because I wanted to. I haven't even kissed a girl since the night I took you home and kissed you before we had to part. My love is yours; I know you can make me the happiest guy in this world. Your letters are making me happy now, and I know you'll make me much happier when we are together. Since you said that you would marry me, it seems we are much closer to one another. We both know of the hardships, but it takes trouble and happiness both to really enjoy life. If I ask you to marry me when I first get home, please turn me down at first. Be sure you love me and I love you. I know it's been a hard task for you to be as true to me as you have. I know you love me, and I love you for it. Our love is for each other. I love your letters and pictures best of all when I can't be with you.

I'm glad you are doing good in school. I don't guess you have many men teachers, do you? I wish I were your teacher; I would keep you after school.

I have to get up at 3:30 in the morning, so will close for now. Write soon, and remember I will always love you.

January 30

My only Sweetheart,

I received your most welcomed letters today. They were dated January 18th and 19th. Robert is up tonight, and we are sitting in the mess hall, so we have the tables for our desk. It's kinda stuffy tonight; we can hear the show from here, but can't understand it clearly. We don't enjoy shows any more; all we do is talk of home. There is very little entertainment out here for us, just the same thing over and over again. Last night Robert and I watched the moon come up over the ocean; it left a pretty shining streak across the water. We talked of home, and just anything we could think of. Nothing to look forward to until we get back.

I got a letter from Ned today. He was telling me what a nice girl you were. He told me about his gal in New York and how people had left Marshall, and the new faces, too.

January 7

My Darling Sweetheart,

I received your package. I was surprised and enjoyed it. Thanks a million for the cake, film and gum. Helen, we get gum out here, so if you can't get very much, keep it for yourself. The peppermint candy was good, too. It didn't last long. Robert helped me eat it.

It's 8:30 p.m. I cut bacon and got things ready for breakfast, then went to the show. It was "Henry Aldrich's Little Secret." I didn't like it, so I left. I was going to write to you anyway. I guess I just had you on my mind as usual. I love you so much that I could cry. I read and reread your letters and pretend you are talking to me. I received two letters also. Send me your senior picture ASAP, and send me a card and announcement also, please. Who knows — I might be there.

February 10

My darling Helen,

It's 8:30 p.m. now. I just finished cutting meat for hamburgers for tomorrow's dinner. I washed up a bit so I could hit the hay, and got to thinking of you, so I had to write. You'll have to excuse this writing because I'm using my knees for a writing desk while sitting on the edge of my cot. One of the dogs here in camp had four little pups. They are five weeks old, and we have one in our tent. He's biting my toes and it really feels funny. He's the cutest thing; he gets tangled around everything. We have to keep him tied up so he won't wander off.

Are you captain of your basketball team? I'm so glad you won. I bet the last game was a thriller. I'd love to see you play. Do you still wear the green or blue gym suits? Ha!

Robert was up tonight. We were going to the show, but I had to work, and it rained anyway. When I was on New Caledonia, I used to go to the show at our camp nearly every night, but that was when I first came overseas. Nothing entertains me now; I'm always thinking of you and home. Just to get a letter from you makes me happy. I'm just waiting for them to send me back to you. Until then all I look forward to is your sweet letters, so keep them flying.

Well, there goes taps and I have to get up at 3:30, so will close, hoping to dream of you.

February 14

Dearest Helen,

Are you still my valentine? The last letter I received from you was dated January 26th, but I received one last night dated February 5th. It seemed so long to wait for a nice letter, but I lived through it. Yes! I love my Missouri girl.

I cleaned my rifle today and did a few other things. We got our vaccinations today. Mine didn't get sore, but Robert's did.

The big question is waiting for you after the war. I hope when I get back I can get stateside duty. Then we could see each other often. I can hardly wait to hold you tight in my arms.

February 18

Darling Helen,

Gee, Helen, it seems ages since I received a letter from you. It's only been a few days, but I love your letters so much. I'm sure lonesome for you tonight. Please try not to worry about me. I'll be back to you and loving you forever.

You asked about Robert in one of your letters. He plans to get a divorce and start life over again. His dad is keeping his little girl. He plans to get married if he can find someone who loves him and his daughter.

February 19

My Darling Helen,

I'm so lonesome for you tonight. I received the sweetest and most welcomed letter of February 8th, and to top that, honey, I got to see the best show. It was "The Great American Romance." Don't miss it if you haven't seen it!

It is 10 p.m. and I have to get up at 3:30, but I love to write to you. You mean so much to me. I could just squeeze you and kiss you forever.

I'm sitting here in the galley writing. Frenchie, the mess sergeant, is writing to a lawyer to get a divorce. This war is bad on life in every way, but, Helen, our plans must and will work out for a happy life together. I've read your letter over and over, trying to picture you talking to me. It would be heaven sitting on the beach with you, watching the moon come up.

Do you remember me calling you a race horse? You didn't like that, did you? Oh, yes! And the ribbon you won.

85

About when I'll be home, I don't know. I have my time in, but there's still another job to do, and the Marines can do it. The Marines that landed 750 miles from Japan weren't us, so don't worry. Remember I'm in the 4th Marines, or 6th Marine Division.

I think sometimes about going back into line duty, packing a rifle. I'll have to fight where I am, but I know how when it's with a rifle. I'll never be sorry for being a rifleman.

It's getting late. I will try to write every chance I get. Write soon, and remember I'll always love you and will be thinking of you wherever I am.

February 22

My Darling forever,

I received four of the sweetest letters from you of January 29th, February 4th, 7th and 9th. Gee, honey, they sure pepped me up. You know what they mean to me.

So Jimmy got married; he doesn't write. The Navy doesn't know what real war is, to have a dirty Jap crawl in the foxhole with you and fight hand to hand.

It seems as though all the girls are getting married. It's okay with me just so I get the one I love so much. Just so some soldier or sailor doesn't beat my time when I'm out here almost helpless, but I trust you, so I don't worry about anything. I'm sending you a picture of myself and a friend. How about a snapshot?

When Paul (my brother) was on Saipan, I asked Captain Ray Luckle to let me fly there to see him, but he said "no." We were getting ready for another invasion.

March 8

My Darling Helen,

Hello, honey. I received so many nice letters from you dated February 15th to the 21st, but have been unable to answer any sooner. I've been thinking of you all the time.

(I told Helen by code, "We are leaving this place,

Dorothy, my brother Paul and Jimmy.

destination unknown, and will be unable to write for some time.")

I would sure love to see you in your new spring suit. Tell your mom thanks for the nice cake, and it meant a lot to me. She's really swell, just like you, always happy. I can hardly wait to get your picture. Please take some pictures of yourself and send them to me. Send me some nice pin-up pictures.

Helen and her mom

Helen

March 12

My Darling,

I wish I was there to keep you company in your apartment. I know you miss Mil. I had to clean the lantern and fill it. We were out of kerosene, so I had to use diesel fuel, and it smokes quite a bit, but I just had to write. Keep this in mind, I'll always love you.

I sent Helen a corsage and potted plant for Easter.

March 12th, we left Guadalcanal for Okinawa, aboard the U.S.S. McIntyre.

U.S.S. McIntyre, 3-12-45 to 4-1-45, Going to Okinawa

March 19

My Helen,

Yes, Helen, I'd love a small picture of you. I haven't received the big one and probably won't for a while. Write me some long letters.

Okinawa, 4-1-45 to 7-6-45

Quote: Easter Sunday, April 1, 1945: "That Easter dawn was hailed by the crash of guns from some 1,200 ships, the largest war fleet that ever sailed, with the heavy artillery of battleships and cruisers concentrating on the sloping ground from the beach to Yontan Airfield 1,200 yards inland."

We hit Okinawa Easter Sunday at Yontan Airfield, without much opposition. We advanced up the northern part of the island. When the interior part of Okinawa was secure, we went south to Naha. We got on land-

Ray on Okinawa after living on rations for three months.

ing crafts and came across the water and hit the Japs from behind the Oroku Peninsula. From there we went down to the southern tip of Okinawa, south of Naha. We were there until the island was secured. We had lived on rations for three months.

April 20, I wrote on Red Cross stationery:

My Dearest Helen,

Hi, honey, here I am writing to you. It's been such a long time. I've been thinking of you every chance I get. I guess you know by now that I'm on Okinawa.

I received letters from you dated March 20th to April 4th. Helen, it's so sweet of you to write me like you have. I can never express what your letters mean to me. You know that I still love you with all my heart. I'll try to write every chance I get. Helen, please send me some pictures soon, just any picture of you, I love them all.

I finally got pencil and paper together so I could write to you. You are the first I've written to for a month.

I guess the guy that was telling you about being in Australia for 18 months thought he had it tough. They say it's swell in New Zealand or Australia.

I'm chewing some good old Juicy Fruit chewing gum. That's

your favorite, isn't it? I had hopes of getting home this summer, but I won't say for sure now. Gosh! I never thought I would get this close to Japan. It's kinda cold up here. There are no coconut trees, but lots of pine trees. My lips are chapped and my face scaled up from the change in weather, but are better now, just right for you to kiss.

Robert Lindsay was wounded on this island. I'll tell you more when I can. He may write to you.

I received a cute card from your mother and the Easter card from you. How about a picture of you in your blue jeans and a T-shirt? I might call you cowboy, too!

I guess you are living with Mildred and Dotty now. I'm feeling fine and think of you all the time.

It's tough about Roosevelt, but we still have a damn Democrat. We need Dewey, don't we?

I'm glad you liked the flowers I sent you for Easter. I thought of you even through all the excitement here.

I better close and write to Mom and Dad. Remember I will always love you. I'll write every chance I get.

Robert Lindsay, my best friend, was shot in the leg and arm, and a toe was shot off in the battle for Mount Yaetake. He was evacuated and sent to Hawaii to the hospital.

The day before Robert was shot, I saw him hiking to the front lines, as we were riding in ammo trucks, pulling 37MM guns. I handed him a can of pineapple juice.

Red Lindsay.

April 30

My Dearest Helen,

I've received several more of your sweet letters, dated March 18th to April 12th. The mail is all screwed up in dates, but gosh, I love to hear from you. My mail will be slow for some time, but when I can write often again, it won't be long 'til "I'll Be Seeing You." I'm still on Okinawa.

Gee, I'm lonesome for you, I love you so much. I know it's hard

89

for you to write when you don't hear from me for two or three weeks, but please keep writing. You know I will write when I can. It makes me feel good to think of being with you soon. It seems like a dream, but it will come true soon, I hope. I keep thinking of all the things we can do.

I would have loved to have seen you in the senior plays. I know you were swell.

In your letter you asked me if I was thinking of my Missouri girl, the one in Marshall. Helen, you know I am always thinking of you. I guess you are wondering about the gal in Carrollton. I haven't told you much about her. I didn't think you wanted to hear that. Yes, I still write to her, but you're always first in everything. She writes quite a bit, but she does good to get a letter once a month from me. She sends me some nice pictures, but I treasure yours more, when you send them. She gets serious but never enters my mind. You hurt me more when you were going with that sailor, but I forgave you, so just forget her.

Yes, I remember May 3rd, 1942. It was Bob McDonough and James Chambers who had the marshmallow fight. I was too busy thinking of you.

I gotta go. I'll write when I can. Oh, yes! I got a notice from Life Magazine that I would receive a copy soon Ha! I'll get most of them in the States, I hope. We can look at them together.

May 7

Hi, Honey,

I have a little time so will let you know I still love you. I received two very sweet letters from you a few days ago, also the swell picture.

I just took off my shoes so my feet could get a bit of air. They get a little raw while in battle.

Well, it won't be long until school is out. I guess you're planning on what you are going to do. I don't know what to tell you. I'll most likely be home in a few months. I'm hoping that we can go swimming, some anyway, and lay out on the grass. Helen, please send me some nice pictures of you in some nice summer dresses. Gosh, honey, you can send me more pictures than you have been. Darling, I want you to know that they mean so much to me.

I can't tell you half what I want to, or what I'm doing. I'm feeling fine and always thinking of you and home. I'm happy that I'm in good health. I don't know how Robert Lindsay is. He was shot in both legs. I'm hoping to hear from him soon.

Write me soon and tell me all about yourself. How much do you weigh now? Don't forget some pictures for your buddy.

May 15

Hi, Honey Bunch,

I received two sweet letters from you a few days ago, but wasn't in the right place to answer them. Gosh, honey, your letters have been slow lately. I realize you have been busy getting ready to gradu-ate, but remember, Helen, I still love to hear from you.

It's pretty cloudy out today. I'm sitting here in the crowded little foxhole trying to look on the brighter side of life while I have a few minutes. I would sure love to be the lucky guy that goes to the junior-senior prom with you. I'd sure love to see you in the new formal Mary gave you. I know you looked sweet in it.

Helen, I'm glad to hear you say you don't care if I write to other girls. That's the only fun I have out here. You're having your fun now, and I'll have mine when I get back.

I guess June will be home soon. The news is really good about Germany, but we have a long fight ahead of us over here. I'm start-ing on my 27th month overseas. I have four battle stars on my cam-paign ribbon, and I have the Navy Citation for Guam.

I still love you and am planning on having some good old times with you when we get together.

Helen says: Marshall, Mo. was a small town at that time (around 8,000). Everyone who knew me knew of (my guy) in the South Pacific. Of course, I dated; there were no secrets in Marshall, and anyway, Ray's sister Dotty was my best friend. Another of his sisters in Marshall, Mildred, was a dear friend. Anyone I dated was very respectful of me, and I appreciated that. They knew they couldn't compete with a Marine overseas, and they said as much. About the end of my senior year I was asked to be engaged (he knew what my answer would be). I was told when we were en-gaged the fraternity would serenade us from the college windows. (It did sound like fun.) Of course, I said "no." My heart was some-where else.

Anyway, Ray wouldn't have loved me if I had stayed home and done nothing. I wouldn't even have liked myself.

The ROTC left Marshall about the time the war ended in Europe. Ray's sister Dotty married an ROTC cadet, Howard Turner. After leaving Marshall, he was stationed at Catalina Island, off California, and Dotty went with him.

May 23

My Dearest Darling,

Gosh, honey! I hit the jackpot. I received three letters from you, one from Mom and Dad, and two from Mil.

I didn't get much sleep last night. My shelter leaked, and I got wet and muddy in this old foxhole, but I just had to write to you even though I'm sleepy. Helen, you'll always mean everything to me. I love you so much.

I'm using a piece of cardboard across my knees for my writing table, and it's pretty hard to write in this position. Excuse the paper — but this is war.

It makes me so happy to hear from you, to know that you are still waiting for me. You are the only one who means anything to me. I may have a few crazy ideas left in my head, but I know when we get together we'll both want to get married. I love you, Helen.

All I can tell you about Robert is that he was shot in both legs. I received a short letter from him the other day. As soon as I receive his new address, I will send it to you. (Excuse the change of paper.) Robert will get to the states soon.

Ray in Okinawa foxhole

Yes, Helen, you and Dot do get some silly ideas when you write your letters together. I'd love to be with you. You could take some of your meanness out on me. I'd like that. All I can do any more is think of being with you. Please write often and send me some pictures.

June 2nd, I wrote on American Red Cross stationery:

My Darling Helen,

I guess you have seen in the paper that we have been pretty busy lately so have been unable to write, but I have thought of you every day.

I washed my clothes yesterday after so long a time. Here I am starting the month off right by writing to you. We had mail call about dark last night. I received so many nice sweet letters from you dated May 8 to the 21st. I love the pictures you sent. The picture of you and Dotty is really good. You look so happy and full of pep. The one in your Easter suit is nice.

All the scenery in the pictures looked natural to me. Oh, how I remember when I used to come out to see you. When we left and came out the front door, I would strip the leaves off the shrubbery

Helen and Dorothy

and throw on you. You looked so nice in all the pictures you sent and so nice in the picture with your mom.

I'm writing this letter in my pup tent. It's hardly big enough to sit up in, but it keeps the wind and rain out — sometimes.

No, Helen, when I left, I didn't think we would be apart this long, but it can't be helped. We still love each other; that's the only thing that counts.

So you're going to stay in Marshall this summer. That is swell of you, but listen, Helen, do what you want. Nothing will keep us apart when I get home.

The little pictures you pasted on your letters were cute, and oh yes, the picture in your bathing suit is a knock-out.

I don't believe I'll like skating when I got back. There are so many other things I have planned for us. It will be swell to take you to dinner and different things. I want to be with you where it is quiet and we can have fun together.

How is the tire and gas situation now? Helen, there has been nothing said about us coming home, but I'm sure counting on it in a few months. It sure makes me feel swell to think about us being together again.

I wish it were possible to send you a picture of me. I will as soon as possible. Keep sending me pictures of you. If you don't, I'll spank you when I get back.

I haven't heard any more from Robert.

I'm glad you decided to stay in Marshall this summer. I'm just hoping I'll be home while it's still warm, so we can be out in your yard under a nice shade tree, where we can talk things over. Only to be with you will be heaven.

June 9th, I wrote on Red Cross stationery:

My Helen,

It is a bright sunny day here on Okinawa. It's early morning. I got up and started a little fire and made some Joe (coffee) for eight of us. We had some bacon and some canned eggs that come in the rations. I washed my face and combed my hair. I feel good now so will write to you, darling. This is the first chance I've had to write for a week, so will take advantage of it. I received mail last night the first for six days. I received two from you and a little note you put with Lee's letter. I enjoyed it, too, just to know you think of me makes me feel swell. Your letters were dated May 23rd and 28th.

I use the little calendar you sent me for Christmas a lot out here. The only date I want to remember is the one with you and lots to follow.

I'll be home by the time June gets there or before if everything goes okay. It's really hard to plan what we will do. So we'll just wait and hope for the best. There's no doubt that we will have the best time possible. There's so much we can do to stir up some excitement.

I'm still in good health and feeling fine. I'm sure lonesome for you.

June 16th, I wrote on Red Cross stationery:

Hi, Honey,

Yes, it's me again thinking of you, darling, as usual, only this is different because I have time to let you know I still love you.

Ray with souvenir Jap flag.

I'm using a Jap pen that I found. I guess you know I'm still on Okinawa. I'm feeling okay. I'm really lonesome for you and your love.

I just finished cleaning my rifle and getting the rest of my gear squared away. I received three letters from you. They were sure sweet. I finally received the large picture of you like the billfold size you sent me.

Do they have crowds at the skating rinks now days? How many times do you fall?

There's nothing been said when we would go home, but surely I'll be home in a few months after this operation is over. I'm sure planning on it, and I have plenty of time over here. I'm just hoping I'll be home while it is still warm so we can lay out on the grass under a nice shade tree and talk to each other. What date is the fair? Gosh, I hope to be home by then. We'll take in everything. We can play cards with Mil and Ray and do so many things to have fun. Only to be with you will be heaven. I could just talk and talk about what I want to do, but will wait 'til I can be with you and plan together. Write soon and often.

June 23rd, I wrote on Red Cross stationery:
My Darling Helen,

Hi, honey, how's everything on the home front? Do you still think of me?

At last this island is secured, but there are still plenty of stray Japs around to mop up. I still won't be able to write very often because of moving around and different things that I can't tell.

I received two letters from you and the card with the long note in it. As you know, they pepped me up. Things get so dull out here, I'm always thinking of you and the good time we'll have together.

I received another letter from Robert. He is in Pearl Harbor in the hospital. I sent him your address so he will write to you.

Gosh, I was surprised to hear you had moved, and that you and Lee were living together. What a pair! What's the address, and do you live upstairs? Have they opened the swimming pool, and have you been?

Helen, it seems like a dream when I think of going home and being with you again.

I received a letter from Ned. He said he might get to see me soon. Here's hoping! Gosh, I'd love to see him and talk about old times.

Helen

Helen, I'm feeling fine, just lonesome for you; it's been so long. I need you and your love, then I'll be the happiest guy in the world.

June 30

My Darling Helen,

It's been some time since I have had time to write. I've been busy. I'll tell you what I've been doing — that is, what will pass the censor.

Guess what! I got to see Ned. I really had a nice visit with him. I asked him about you. It really made me feel good, he said so many nice things that make me proud of you.

(Ned said, "The first thing Raymond asked me was "How's Helen?" And I hadn't seen her for months, but then he hadn't seen her for 2-1/2 years.)

Ned stayed all night with me. He slept in the foxhole with me for his first time in a foxhole. He also took a bath with me. We had a water shortage, so he had to wash with two gallons of water and so did I. I gave him some Jap money and showed him my Jap flags and different things. Gosh! It was swell to see him. I nearly beat him to death, I was so glad to see him. I'm going to see him tomorrow on his ship.

It's about 8:30 p.m. It's too hot in the daytime to try to write; also I have to work.

My brother's ship docked somewhere close to the Naha Airport. He remembers crossing the airfield when he was looking for me. He found me at Itoman. His captain had told him he could come ashore at his own risk. He hitchhiked to where I was. We were set up in a circular defense, and he came in about 4 p.m.

Nelson stayed all night and slept in my foxhole. The first thing he wanted to know was why I didn't dig it deeper. I had to stand guard an hour to keep the Japs from creeping up on us. That was from 12 to 1 a.m. When I got off guard duty, he was awake and we talked until the other fellow got off at 2 a.m., and

Ray and Nelson on ship.

then we went to sleep. The mosquitoes really bit him; he couldn't sleep very well.

We talked a lot. Per Nelson's letter to Mom and Pop, "We talked worse than two old maids."

I got permission to go back to Nelson's ship with him and spend the night. We caught a truck ride to the ship. It was nice to have a good hot meal and a bed.

Dearest Helen,

I really had a nice visit with Nelson. I asked him about you. It made me feel good, it was swell to see him. We tried to talk about everything at once. We have moved to a different area since I saw him. We have been fixing up a place to sleep and a galley to put out "chow" for the guys. We will try to cook some now after three months of living on rations. I'm using a flashlight to write this letter. Tell Mom and Dad you heard from me.

After Nelson left, we went out on patrols. I was carrying explosives for the demolition crew. If we thought there were Japs in the brush piles, we would throw grenades into them. When we found a cave, we would holler, "Come out," in Japanese. If they didn't come out, we blasted the cave shut. One patrol jumped up three Japs, and they shot at them as they were going over a hill. Later the three Japs came back over the hill waving a white flag to surrender. We continued the day, carrying the 60-80# explosive packs.

Dearest Helen,

Oh yes! I made another rate. I was lucky to get it. That makes me Chief Cook, a Staff Sergeant rate, a little more money, too.

I received three of the sweetest letters from you dated June 13th, 17th and 18th. I love you so much.

Okay, so we won't worry about the gas and tires. I got a big laugh when you were telling about us having a blow-out. We'll be happy, just so we're together.

I'm using a flashlight to write this letter, so excuse the mistakes.

Helen, I want to be with you so bad, I can't stand it much longer.

Tell Mom and Dad you heard from me. I'll write again in a few days. I love you always.

I started addressing Helen's letters to Cut Price Clothing Store, June 30th, where she was working.

The four stars on my campaign ribbon are for Bougainville, Emirau, Guam and Okinawa, and the Navy Citation for Guam.

July 2

My Helen,

I just finished writing to my folks and Mildred. I was thinking of you so just had to drop you a line.

I went out to see Ned yesterday and stayed all night with him. We had a nice visit. He said you hadn't changed any, said you were really nice, but I already knew that.

I received the picture you sent in your last letter. Thanks a million, Helen. I love it. I'm looking at it now. I have you in my left hand, so don't try to get away.

So buying hats is your weakness. Well, hon, you're mine. I like the hat you have on with your Easter outfit.

I often wonder if we'll get married when I get back. It would be wonderful, but I'd like to wait 'til after the war.

Which side of the street do you live on? Draw me a picture of your room, and how to get to it. I might come to see you in two or three months. How would you like that, Helen?

You make me hungry when you tell me about those bacon and

tomato sandwiches. I wish I were there, too. What a time we could have. Can you get a vacation when I get back? I want to be with you as much as possible, if it's okay with you, darling. Write soon and often.

LST, 7-6-45 to 7-16-45

We went on patrols "mopping up" and then went back to Guam for **more** training. We left Okinawa July 6th aboard LST 1110 for Guam. It was 1200 miles.

Guam, 7-16-45 to 8-15-45

July 17

My Darling Helen,

The last letter I wrote to you was July 2nd. I hope you forgive me; I've been unable to write to anyone. I received two letters from you about two weeks ago dated June 22nd and 24th. I sure enjoyed them; they mean so much to me.

I can hardly wait to be with you again and hold you in my arms, to look into your beautiful blue-green eyes (Oh! Oh! Something wrong here, I thought. It stumped me for a minute, then I looked up the code I had sent Ray, and blue-green meant he was on Guam. Thank goodness, he didn't get me mixed up with another girl friend.)

Well, Helen, how do you like your new job at Rose & Buckners? How did the bathing beauty contest come out? Again, I wish I could have been the judge. I'm so proud of you, I love you.

It just does something to me when you tell me about going out to your folks. Oh! I can just smell the red roses and the honeysuckle now, just as if I were with you. Maybe it won't be long now. Gosh, it's been a long time, hasn't it?

I hope to get some mail soon. I'm sending you a picture of Ned and me. You've probably already seen the ones that Ned sent to Mom and Dad, but I was unable to send it sooner.

I hope I get your letters soon. I should get a lot of mail, I hope. Write soon.

I started addressing Helen's letters to Rose & Buckner's, where she is now working, July 21st. It is a men's clothing store, women's accessories and men and women's shoes. She works upstairs in the back of the store in the office with Anna Belle Halsey. It is an open office, so they can see the bottom floor and the front door. When the mail man brings a letter for either of them from their boyfriend, he yells upstairs to tell them they got a letter.

July 21

My Helen,

I know my mail has been slow, but I can't help it. I'll try to do better, and I might even see you in two months or so. I don't know yet, still waiting.

I received your letters dated June 26 to July 11th. You're still my darling.

Yes, I know Charlie McGraw. Where is he now?

Say, honey, how about a nice pair of liberty shoes when I get back? I'll even let you sell them to me.

Robert Lindsay is in the States now, in Oakland, California, with both legs in casts. He's getting along fine. He said he would write to you.

How much do you weigh now, and how tall are you? Please answer.

Yes, Helen, I remember all about you and the fun we had together, and how swell you have been to me since I've been over here. It all adds up to I love you very much.

It's so hard for me to write any more, even to you. All I can think of is being with you. I just sit and dream of you and me together again. Darling, your letter of the 9th of July was sure sweet and just like you. You seemed so happy while writing it. I love you.

Yes, Helen, I know right where you live by the illustration you sent. I'll be sure to look you up. I don't know whether to surprise you or not.

I'm hoping to hear from you often. I'm still in good health.

July 27

Dearest Helen,

Well, here it is the last of July, and I'm still out here, thinking of you and wishing I was with you. It's 6 p.m. and the mosquitos haven't started biting, but will before long.

Guess what, Helen! Ned came to see me yesterday about 9 o'clock. This time on Guam. I was sure glad to see him again. It had only been 20 days since I last saw him, but it was much more pleasant this time because of the surroundings. I was on duty, but we had a swell talk. I gave him my Jap rifle. He will keep it or send it home.

So Friday 13th used to be lucky for you. I don't know which it is for me. I was on the ship and, believe me, I kept away from the sides.

You and Mil are getting to be good skating partners, I bet. "Chattanooga Choo Choo" sounds like a good song to skate to. Oh, how I would love to skate with you in the moonlight skate.

Your letter of the 17th was when you and Mil were at Hansbros, that was my latest letter.

The time is really passing slow for me now, waiting to be with you again.

Darling, I'll be so happy when we can be out at your folks. It will be like the good old days, and bring back so many memories of you. Just think, Helen, it's almost four years since we first started going together. I can hardly wait to see you. You mean everything to me. I'll always love you.

I'm going to drop Mil a line. I'm still pretty busy around here. I haven't been to a show for a long time. Write often.

We were training again for the next invasion — Japan, but I was sure hoping for a ship to come home on.

August 3

Hi, Honey,

I received two of the sweetest letters from you tonight. Oh, they were swell! Darling, you sound so happy, and I know just how you feel. I was just as happy three weeks ago because I thought I'd be right home, but it looks like I'll be here for a month or two now. I sure hate to tell you that, but still, Helen, it won't be long. We'll just have to stick it out 'til we are together again. I guess you have heard from me by now. I sure hope so. My mail has been slow lately. Helen, please keep writing often. I need your letters more now that I'm so close to getting to be with you. I love you, Helen.

It's sure hard for me out here now, just working and waiting for them to give me the word to go to the good old States and be with you. All I think of is you, and us being so happy together.

Have you head from Robert? He is in Memphis, Tennessee now. Just add Naval Hospital to his address. He will love to hear from you, and so do I.

I hope to be home soon.

Helen, I think it will be swell if you could go to Washington, D.C. with Mary. You've waited so long on me. I'm always in your way. I do hope I get my leave before you go though. I'll try to get stationed in "Philly," Penn. when I get back, so you see we will be close to each other.

I'm still feeling okay, honey, just blue and lonely for you.

Helen, I fell in love with the two letters I received tonight from you. Oh, you sounded so sweet and happy. I know you love me and that makes me feel so good and, Helen, you know that I'm deeply in love with you. Please keep writing to me often. I hope to see you soon.

August 10

My Darling Helen,

Gosh, Helen, I haven't heard from you for ages, are you still okay? I know you think I'm on the way home. I hate to tell you this, but I'm still out here, waiting for the chance. I don't know when that will be. It's sure hard on me thinking about all the swell things I could be doing at home and with you, darling. I know it's hard on you and the folks, too, but it can't be helped. There is no transportation, they say, but I don't believe that. I start on 30 months overseas tomorrow.

Well, Helen, I'll tell you what I have been doing. I've been working hard. We cook for 600 men now. It really keeps me busy — believe me.

Boy, I sure hope I hear from you tomorrow, Helen. It makes the days so long and nothing to look forward to when I don't hear from you, sweetheart. I know it's hard for you to write, but please try, Helen, and I'll try to do better.

I just heard the news of the world. It sure sounds good; I don't think it will be much longer. I didn't get to hear the President's talk today, but some of the guys told me what it was about.

I take back what I said about Harry Truman. He turned out to be the perfect President, just what we needed.

Helen, there's sure no news here. All I can think of is being with *you and the good times we used to have, makes me lonesome for you. I love you, Helen, so please write soon and often.*

August 14, 1945, Japan surrendered. I was in bed when the news came. We had a small radio in our tent, and we left it on all night to get the details.

I got up at 4 a.m. the next morning to cook. The war still wasn't officially over, but everyone seemed happy.

That afternoon we had orders to be ready to ship out in 48 hours, so everyone was real busy. We got all new equipment just like we were going to have a parade. All the trucks had to be painted.

U.S.S. Grimes, 8-15-45 to 8-30-45

We got aboard ship, the U.S.S. Grimes, August 15th, and headed for Japan.

Helen writes:

August 24

I attended my Uncle Henry Gregg's military funeral in Independence, Mo. He was a WWI veteran, and had served in Siberia as a night guard. As we started home, we noticed people on their porches waving flags and ringing bells. We knew then that the war had ended. I decided right then that I wanted to stay in Kansas City with Mary, so Mom and Dad took us to Mary's apartment. (Actually it was just a sleeping room with no place to cook or eat.) Mary and I then rode the streetcar downtown and joined in the celebration. What a great feeling! The war was finally over!

All the stores and eating places were closed. People emerged from everywhere. For six blocks everyone was jammed so closely together we could hardly move, and you certainly had to go the direction the crowd was going. There were many servicemen in the crowd; everyone was shouting, laughing, yelling, singing and kissing. Merry-makers in Hotel Phillips emptied feathers from the pillows in the rooms. The feathers were accompanied by paper and confetti from surrounding buildings. It looked like a snowstorm. There was also some water being thrown from the windows, but no one seemed to mind.

K.C. Star picture — "A Joyful Moment in the History of Kansas City"
*— Wednesday Times, August 25, 1945. **That's Helen where circle is.***

We were hungry, but there was no place to eat. Finally the crowd moved past a Penny Arcade, and we were able to get some popcorn and artificial orange juice there.

I had on new black patent leather high heel shoes that I had worn to the funeral and a little white hat. My feet were killing me, but I didn't care. We finally did find some steps to sit on to rest a couple of minutes. It was a great celebration, and a memory that lasts forever.

August 24

My Darling Helen,
I've been thinking of you, although I have been unable to write. Guess what! This part was censored (cut out of the letter), but it

probably said: "They found a ship that I had always hoped for so long, but I'm headed in the wrong direction."

By the time you receive this letter, you will know where I am. We are going to represent the Old Fourth Regiment in Japan. (There were 120 members of the Old 4th liberated from the Philippines when the war ended.)

Helen, I hated to tell you this. I know you had swell plans for us. Boy, it was sure a let-down to me. Just think, darling, I had my sea bag all packed and all ready to go home to be with you again, which I've been planning on since we parted.

I'm really disgusted with everything over here, but I still have something to look forward to.

Yes, Helen, the war is over, and I'm so happy for everyone. I know everyone at home is happy, too. It's really a great feeling, but it sure screwed me up getting home when I planned to be. Gosh, Helen, look how long you have waited and planned so much for us. I've had to wait, too, but I had to; I had no other choice. How can I ever express my love for you, darling? You've been so swell to me, Helen. I just hope and pray that it won't be too long until we can be together again forever. Helen, this is the way I feel at present. I'm really disgusted with everything over here. Thirty months over here, and nothing to look forward to. I want to be with you so bad it nearly drives me nuts, but I guess I'll live through it. Helen, it's up to you now; do whatever you decide to do or your feelings tell you to. I don't feel I should ask you to wait any longer unless you wish to. I can tell you truthfully that you are the only girl that I love or care anything about. I quit writing to Lora Lee four months ago, because I had made up my mind that you are the one and only for me.

I can hardly wait now to see if we are still going to get married. I know I love you enough, but you can never tell what will come up. Gosh, it seems ages since I heard from you. What are your plans now? Have you changed your mind? Write me a real long letter; let me know just how you feel.

Just think, all the guys will be home again soon — all my old buddies, Jim, Bob, Shorty and me together again. I plan on one or two good times with them again, just to celebrate old times. Gosh, to think that Bob and Jimmy are married, and to think about it, it could happen to me — I hope.

Boy, it's sure hard to plan on anything, isn't it, Helen? But when we are together again, the plans we make will work out. I'll always love you.

It's sure hot in the compartments of this ship, and to think of sleeping down here makes me sweat.

I wonder what you are doing tonight. It's nice and warm where you are and so peaceful. If only I were there with you, darling, we could be so happy. It will be swell to dance with you again, after you teach me. Just a month ago I thought sure we would be together by now. I'm really disappointed, and I know how you must feel, but I still have something to look forward to. Tell everyone hello, and be sure to write me a long letter. Be good.

Japan, 8-30-45 to 11-3-45

In three days we were close to Japan, but we sailed back and forth just out of the harbor. We anchored in the bay for two days, then landed the morning of the 31st. So here I am.

We could see Mt. Fuji as we came into the bay. It was some sight to see. The Japs left the Naval base pretty clean. There were two or three Japs on the beach taking pictures of the landing. It sure seemed good to land so peacefully.

We pulled into the harbor of Japan at Yokosuka Naval Base. As a member of the Tokyo occupation force, I participated in the initial landing and occupation of the Yokosuka Bay area.

We went ashore unopposed at Yokosuka Naval Base. We were locked in the base with guards on the gate. It wasn't long until some of the guys got some old Jap trucks and motorcycles running. There were some rowboats that weren't locked up, so some of the guys got in those and got around the guards and got out of the base. After that the boats were chained up. Then some of the guys put their clothes in a barrel, and after they were around the guards, they changed clothes and went ashore.

September 3

My Darling Helen,

At last I'll try to answer your letters of July 30 and August 1st. Everything's been happening so fast, it's hard to keep up with myself. I'm at Yokosuka Naval Base. Everything seems peaceful and going along okay. It seems funny to be here in Japan and not be fighting. I'm glad of that! Well, the war is over, so when I get back, I won't have to come back over here.

I am now cooking for 1000 men.

It seems ages since I received a letter. Everyone quit writing because they thought I was on the way home. I should get some letters in a few days — I hope.

It's hard to believe we are so far apart after planning on being together for so long.

Yes, here I am, sitting on a Jap double bed in their barracks writing to you. I'm on the top sack.

I received a roll of film you sent, so will snap a few shots of Japan for you.

It really gets chilly here. I can sleep good in this weather. I have to use a blanket, too.

This place hasn't been bombed, so it's in good condition. I was sure surprised. You see lots of Marines driving Jap cars and trucks around that are here on the base. I haven't been around much yet, so haven't seen many Japs.

Darling, I'm still planning on the day we can be together again. I still love you as always, Helen. I sure hope I receive a letter from you soon. I'm so lonesome for you. It's hard to express my feelings in a letter. I just hope and pray that it won't be too much longer. We have so much to talk over with each other. Write often.

I received a nice letter from Dorothy. Gosh, it was a surprise, and it's hard to believe that she's married. I haven't heard from home, so I didn't know Mildred was operated on. I hope she puts on some weight now.

September 8

My Darling Helen,

At last my mail caught up with me, and now I'm happy. I received several letters from you and from home.

They finally lifted the censorship for us, so will answer your questions now, and I'll try to write a more interesting letter. Just give me time to get used to it.

This will be the first letter I have sealed since I've been over here. The letters I received from you were dated August 5th to the 21st. I sure enjoyed them and to know you still love me and are waiting 'til we are together again.

I don't know what they have planned for the regiment, but I hear talk that we might go to China, and then to the States. I'll write as often as possible while I'm here. It's impossible to write while aboard ship, please remember that.

I'm glad June is getting back soon. I wish I could also be there then; we could have so much fun. It's hard to say when I'll get home, but it can't be too long, I know.

I wanted to be home round this time so bad, because it would still be nice weather, and we could have had so much fun. I guess I'll see some snow when I get back now, but we'll still have the time of our lives, won't we, Helen?

Helen, I've always been in the Marine Corps Reserve. I didn't want to sign up for four years; that would be too long to be away from you. I sure didn't think we would be apart so long when I joined. I'm glad I didn't know that, or I would have gone nuts. This way I always say that I'll see you in a few months, but it seems someone keeps putting it off.

Yes, darling, I'm still cooking for about a thousand men. It keeps me busy, but the time passes faster for me that way.

Here it is about time for school to start again, but you don't have to think about that this year.

Do you plan to keep working, or do you find it hard to plan anything? I haven't planned on anything too strong. My plans are built around you, and if they don't work out, no telling what I'll do. It looks to us guys out here that we are going to be out of work. But I think I can make a fair living. If a guy is willing to work, he can always get by.

Helen, did you have a nice vacation? Your uncle died, and the war ended during the funeral. I wish I could have been home during your vacation. What a time we could have had! I guess all the people in the States really celebrated when the war ended. We didn't celebrate; I was in bed when the news came. We had a small radio in our tent, and we left it on all night to get the details. I got up at 4 the next morning to cook. It still wasn't officially over, but everyone seemed happy.

Remember I still love you and always will.

September 14

Hello, Darling,

Here I am perched on my "sack" thinking of you. I just finished taking a shower, and boy, was it cold, but it made me feel good anyway.

Well, Helen, there are about 20 fellows leaving us tomorrow to be discharged. Most of them deserve it, but there are always a few who get the breaks, like one fellow who has just been over here eight months and is getting out. This guy had kids. Some of the others were married and had kids. Most of the guys have been here 30 months or more. I have plenty of points, but I have to wait my turn.

I've seen so many fellows come and go since I have been over here. I guess I'll get a break some day, and then we'll be happy.

I received your letter of August 23rd and was thrilled to hear from you, honey. Thanks a million for the pictures. I'll send you some more pictures in the future.

I'm glad you got to go to the fair. I know you had a good time. Darling, if only we could be together, it's been so long, it will really seem strange, won't it? But the fun we can have! Oh, Helen, I still love you and always will. You're so swell. I sure hope we can get along and get married. I'd be so happy to be with you all the time. Helen, I'll be home some day; please don't give up. I know it's hard for you, but please think how bad it is for me.

Has June made it home? I sure hope so. He and Mary deserve to enjoy married life again.

Helen, write me some real long letters. I love them so. Write soon and often.

September 18

Hi, Honey,

I'm so lonesome for you, Helen. I hope you are writing to me tonight. Oh, how I wish you were in my arms. I love you more than words can say.

I hope you have received some letters from me explaining why my letters are so slow.

I received two letters and a card from you, but they don't mean much to me because you haven't heard from me, so I'll be sure to write when I can. Helen, you know that I still love you and think of you day and night. Please remember that, darling.

I feel like I'm catching a bad cold. This water is so cold to wash in — almost like ice.

I wonder what you are doing tonight. Gosh, it would be swell to be with you. If my plans had only worked out, we could have been lying out in the yard on the nice green grass. I'm still planning for

Mt. Fuji.

us, Helen; I'll never give up hope. Some day we will be happy together.

We were issued a Jap rifle today as a souvenir.

Helen, I'll tell you all I know about this place, as I see it. We pulled into Tokyo Bay the 27th of August and anchored in the bay for two days. Everything seemed peaceful. We could see Mt. Fuji from the ship. It is big and a beautiful sight to see. We looked through field glasses to see things on the beach. After two days we pulled farther into the bay and landed.

They pay us here in "yen." Fifteen yen is equal to our dollar. There are lots of Japs around this base, but they can't get in. They still dress in their uniforms, but are unarmed. They are polite; it seems funny to rub shoulders with them now, when we walk down the street.

We don't get out of the base very often. Everything the Japs have seems to be worn out. You can tell that the war has really been hard on them. I believe they realize that they lost the war.

Are there many boys getting out of the service now? Can you tell it in Marshall?

Ray in Japan.

The letters I received from you were dated Sept. 2nd and 5th. Sure enjoyed your letters, honey, to know that you still think of me.

So you're reading "Forever Amber." All the boys have been reading it. It's hard to get a copy. I haven't read it, but have heard a lot about it. The girl who wrote it, her husband was in our outfit and was wounded on Okinawa. Amber must be some girl! How do you like it?

I am still waiting for a letter from you saying you have heard from me. It will be much easier to write then. Ask me questions that you want to know. Write often. I love you, Helen.

Ray and Goebel.

We had an NCO Club at the base. The enlisted men built a bar in the barracks; it was shaped like the bow of a ship, V-shaped. It was a place for them to loaf and drink beer.

I met and got acquainted with Y. Masuda, a very nice Japanese man. He wanted to show us Japan. He invited Goebel and me to Kamakura, a city of temples and shrines, and to his home.

Ray and Y. Masuda.

Goebel, Ray and Japanese girls.

We took off our shoes before we went into his home, and we drank green tea. It was an all-day trip. We took an old train that had the bottom rotted out. He paid our fare. He invited some Japanese girls to walk with us, and we went to Tokyo Bay and watched people pulling in their fishing nets. He gave us some pictures of Mt. Fuji.

September 24
My Darling Helen,
   Our company converted to an MP company, just to keep the guys out of trouble. I'm still cooking; I

Goebel, Y. Masuda, Ray and Japanese girls.

get up at 3:45 a.m., and a hard day ahead of me. I'll be glad to get out of here, the smell is really bad.

When you go into some of the stores, you have to take your shoes off. It's an old Japanese custom.

How's everything in Marshall these days? Do you still love me a little? Are you writing to me tonight and often? I sure hope so. I love you so much, so please write often, and how about a few snapshots or a small picture. I'd sure love one, Helen. I received two letters from you dated September 7th and 11th; I enjoyed them. Your letters mean everything to me.

When I wrote my letter of August 24th, I thought it wouldn't be censored, but I guess it was. Well, I guess I said I was aboard ship and headed for Japan. That's about all.

I received two letters from Mom today, and she said Lee heard on the radio that the 4th Marines would be home by the middle of October. I hope they meant the 4th Regiment. The talk around here sounds pretty good, but we better get on the way if we get back that soon. I plan on nothing any more; I just hope for the best. It doesn't pay to plan.

Yes, Helen, I do think we will be married because we love each other lots. It seems that we were meant for each other. Gosh, what will it be like being together again? Oh, darling, I love you. We'll be so happy being together. It will be a dream to me, but a swell one.

Most of the Japanese people seem friendly around here, but it pays to be careful. The sailors get to go ashore here now; they buy a lot of trinkets and junk.

I'm enclosing another picture of me. I hope you still love me when you see it. Write soon.

October 8

My Darling Helen,

It's been sometime since I wrote to you. I have no excuse for it, so I won't try to make any. I don't know what's wrong with me. It seems I never get around to writing. I don't take advantage of the time I have. I guess I have "writer's cramps" as you call it. I'll try my best to do better.

I feel good today. I received several letters from you. The latest was dated September 26th. It was swell to hear from you.

Now, to let you know what I've been doing lately. The first thing is to let you know I might be home before long for good. I have 83 points, and all men with 70 points or more have their names turned in for discharge. They tell us our replacements are on the way up here from Guam. I sure hope so, but you know how many times I have been disappointed, and you, too. I'd sure like to believe it, but you know I have a doubt in my mind. You know and I know they can't keep me over here forever, because I don't have my name on that dotted line.

Now to let you know what's going on over here at the Naval Base where the 4th Marines are. Every company gets ten Jap laborers to do the dirty work that we used to do. They clean the barracks and haul trash, wash the pots that I dirty, which the Marine messmen used to do. They also keep the galley clean, working from 7 a.m. until 4 p.m. So that leaves one meal for the messmen to do. The Japanese will do anything for you, and work very hard. Most of them were soldiers, I think. They try to learn English, and we try to learn a few words of Japanese — it's hard to learn.

There are several Japanese interpreters around, too. I sure like to talk to them. They let us know what the Japs think of the war being over; they say most of them are very glad.

When you tell them you were on Okinawa, their eyes pop out, and they say "Okinawa!" They all know about that place. I guess they wonder how we lived through it.

Oh, Helen, if you only knew what I want to tell you. There are so many things, but you probably wouldn't want to hear them. I might tell you some day though.

Just like I heard now. I'm sitting here at the window, and some sailors came by drunk coming from liberty, I guess. There were some Japanese workmen up the road about 50 yards, just getting off work here. One of the sailors was talking how he would like to get hold of him — damn, that makes me mad! The sailor probably just came into the Navy and would run so fast if he had met up with him before the war ended.

I'm sure disgusted. I'll be so happy to be home with you again, darling. I'll probably tell you some stories when I get back. I know a lot of them, but I might not talk about them. No telling what I'll do 'til I get there, ha!

I bet little Dotty was cute in the grass skirt her daddy gave her. I know it was nice if he got it in Hawaii. I would sure have liked to get you a nice one, but couldn't.

Helen, you're swell to write to me like you do. I don't know what

I'd do without your letters. I love you so much. You seem to have a pretty busy life nowdays. I'm glad for you. You seem much happier. I know you're keeping good company, too. Who are some of the boys that are lucky enough to go with you? Kinda nosy, aren't I?

Thanks a million for sending me the box of candy and the film. I only wish you had kept the film and sent me some pictures of you, honey.

No, Helen, I don't know what ship I will come home on, but any of them will be good. I would even hang on the anchor chain, so I can be with you. I don't think I will go to China now.

Helen, I know you have fun bowling, and it's a good clean game. I went to Yokahama the other night; it is really burned out. People live in little tin shacks that they built out of the tin that was left.

Remember, darling, I love you with all my heart. I'm thinking of you always.

October 10

Hello, Honey,

It's getting chilly here now. It's been raining the last two days. We haven't any means of heating these barracks. I hope I'm not here long enough to get very cold, but I'm sure to see some cold weather somewhere between here and the States. Just think — maybe a snowball fight with you.

For entertainment over here we still have the show. I haven't been for so long though. I don't enjoy them without you. The other night we had some Jap boxers put on a few bouts for us; they were good for their size. Oh, yes, we have a beer hall here for Sailors and Marines. Some of the boys really put it away. I got to feeling good a time or two. I still don't like the taste, just drink to feel good with my buddies once in a while.

Helen, what type of clothes are most of the boys wearing now that are out of the service? Have styles changed much? Gee, it will be swell to be a civilian again.

Yes, I knew the girl's husband who wrote "Forever Amber." He was a lieutenant.

Is your mailman Ben Berg?

We got a piece of paper to show we were here in Japan, kind of like a certificate. It's pretty nice.

We finally started getting fresh meat over here. We had chicken the other day, and we had steak three days in a row. It tasted good for a change.

All I can think about is getting home to you. You're the only one I love. Write soon.

October 12

Hello, Honey,

Here it is 10:30 p.m. I just got back from the show, "Her Highness and the Bell Boy." I went with a couple of buddies. I'm glad you told me to see it if I had a chance. It's the first show I've seen since I went a few times aboard the LST taking us to Guam from Okinawa.

Yes, Helen, that show tonight proved to me that I still had a soft spot in my stomach. I had a few good laughs, too, that helped out. If we could only have seen it together!

I'm so lonesome for you. I'll never forget the night I took you to see "The Pride of the Yankees." It was at the Mary Lou Theater, and we sat in the balcony. Do you remember the rest? You know, a few tears. Ha!

Helen, it won't be long now. I sure hope we get along swell. I need your love as bad as you need mine. I do believe we have both changed in the three years we have been apart, but I believe we have changed together, and still love each other. It seems so long since I have heard from you. I know it's not your fault; it's been bad weather here lately and they have been unable to get the mail from the ships. I'll be so happy when we have mail call again. I know I'll hear from you. You're sure swell to write to me like you do.

Oh, yes, the band played for us before the show. It was swell, too, but it made me lonesome for everyone. I've just been out here too long, I believe.

I have to get up at 4 a.m. I hope I dream of you. I hope to see you soon. My fingers are still crossed.

October 17

Hello, Darling,

Damn, it seems that I'm stranded out here forever, and there isn't a damn thing I can do about it. It's sure tiresome, believe me. Your letters are the only thing I live for. Oh, Helen, I still love you, you're so sweet.

Helen, I'd sure love to see yours and Anna Belle's apartment. I know it's really cute. I wish it was ours, wouldn't we be happy though? Yes, I know Anna Belle.

I just finished a letter to Mom and Dad. It had been so long since I had written them. My mail is sure slow.

Thanks a million for the little picture. You know I treasure your

115

pictures very much.

My life out here is so dull at times, always thinking of you and wishing we were together. I have really seen some funny things since I have been here. It's exciting to see some of the things that are here. I don't guess I'll ever regret it after I get home, but I'm sure tired of this life now. Helen, write real often. Remember, I'll always love you.

November 3

My Darling Helen,

Helen! I have some good news for you at last! Yes, I'm on the way home to be with you. I'm so happy I can hardly write. We go aboard an aircraft carrier tomorrow at 1:00. I think we will land in Washington state, but I don't know for sure.

All I can think about is you and my folks. Oh, how happy I'll be, darling. I've been real busy lately, just waiting for this time to come.

We took our physical exams yesterday. I passed it okay. We had to have 28 months over here and over 70 points to make this list; there were very few who made it.

I have received several letters from you, so will answer the most important questions. I want to write to the folks, too.

I hope your mother's knee is better. Tell her she'd better be up and around when I get back.

I hope to get to see Dot and Howard in California, but I have my doubts. I'll do my best to see them.

I'll be thinking of you always.

U.S.S. Calvert to Hawaii and San Francisco, 11-3-45 to 11-22-45

Finally on November 3rd we left Japan aboard the U.S.S. Calvert headed for the USA.

I was helping the Navy cooks on the ship coming home. We had lamb chops in a 15-gallon pot on the deck of the galley. The sea was rough, and they were sliding from one side of the galley to the other. We had to tie them down, and the pans were all falling off the shelves. We did get the lamb chops cooked. We had to have a shirt on in the galley, and we would come out of there wringing wet from the heat.

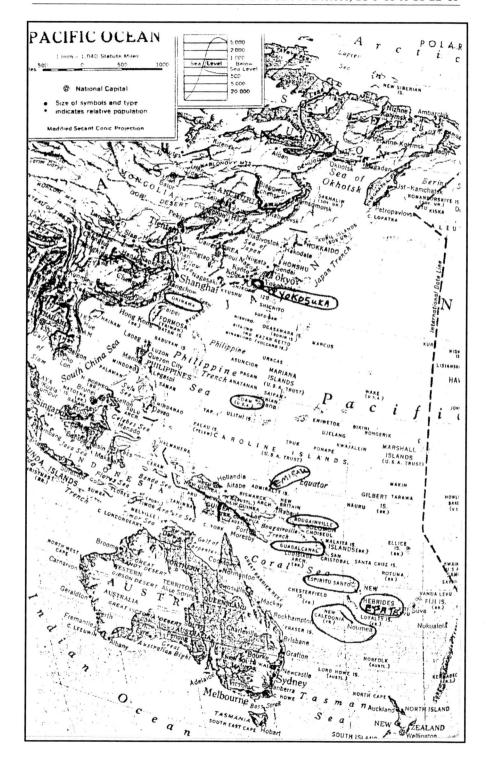

November 11

My Darling, Helen,

I'm headed for the good old States. O, boy! I received your letter of October 24th. I sure enjoyed it. Yes! I should be home by Christmas. We should be in Pearl Harbor by the 15th and be in the U.S.A. by the 25th of the month.

I hope I get to mail this at Pearl Harbor. I'm glad Ed will be home soon, too.

I can't get you off my mind. I'm planning on all the fun we're going to have

George Bucci, Ray, Charol Swanstrom on ship home.

and how happy we will be. I sure hope everything plans out okay for us.

Everything here is going swell, but time really goes slow now. Tonight we will cross the International Dateline, so it will be the same date tomorrow, so see — time doesn't pass for us.

I think we'll be in Pearl Harbor two or three days. I just hope they don't let us off there.

I just got off work and took a shower. I feel really good. Yep! They got me cooking again.

At last I'm aboard ship that doesn't have a blackout at night; it sure seems great. If I get off at Pearl Harbor, I'll send you and Mom a telegraph, if possible. Remember, Helen, I love you with all my heart.

U.S.S. Calvert, between Hawaii and the U.S.A.

November 16

My Dearest, Sweetheart,

Well, honey, we pulled into Pearl Harbor at 3 p.m. We got liberty at 4 p.m. It seemed good to be in civilization again. I was so excited! Four of my buddies and I went together. We drank malted milk and plain milk 'til we were so full. Oh, oh! And ate and ate different things. We went into Honolulu. It's pretty nice there, just like a big carnival, a serviceman's city.

Very few girls, but it sure made a guy want to get back to his girl.

We pulled out of Pearl Harbor at 2 p.m. this day; sure glad we didn't stay any longer.

I just came down from topside; the moon was shining bright. It made me lonesome for you, Helen. I was talking to some of my buddies about civilian life. It will be so nice, I know.

Write me some letters because I don't know how long I'll be in San Diego. Just address it to the R & R Center, San Diego, California.

I'm going to hit the canvas and hope I dream of you. Remember, I love you and will be with you soon.

November 22nd, Thanksgiving Day, we went under the Golden Gate Bridge and to the harbor, then took a bus to Treasure Island, where I sent Helen a telegram. I had spent 156 days aboard ships.

(Helen says: I was at my Mom and Dad's Thanksgiving Day with all the family when I noticed in the *Kansas City Star* the list of troop arrivals at San Francisco. The U.S.S. Calvert was listed. I was so excited! I had to go back to my apartment in the afternoon because I knew Ray would call me. He called at 7 a.m. November 23rd. What a relief that he was back in the U.S.A.)

We laid around all day waiting for a train home, not knowing if we had time to wash out a pair of socks. At night we would go to San Francisco and Oakland.

Troop Train to Chicago

We went by troop train to Chicago. On the side of the train someone had written, "We took Okinawa and Japan, and Frisco took us — $$$.

They thought they were doing me a favor putting me in charge of cooking on the train. We had an old coal stove that we shoved coal into with a flat piece of wood. We made coffee in a 15-gallon open pot, and it would slosh out. Everyone thought they were civilians and didn't want to work. Every time the train stopped, they would jump off the train and run to find a liquor store. One of the guys cut his hand cutting up lettuce for salad.

We arrived in Chicago December 10th and were discharged the same day. I called Helen from Chicago December 11th (my birthday) at 11 p.m.

Train — Chicago to Marshall, Missouri

I left Chicago by train about noon December 12th. I was up all night, too excited to sleep. It as a long night until daybreak. When we went through Slater, Missouri, I knew we were getting close.

I arrived in Marshall, Missouri, December 13th, 1945, at 8 a.m. It was snowing big beautiful snowflakes when my family and Helen walked to the Marshall Depot to meet me. We walked back to Mil and Ray's home at 564 N. Benton Street in the snow. What a wonderful day!

"Let it snow! Let it snow! Let it snow!"

All branches of the service did a terrific job to win the war. Gung Ho!

Ray and Helen

Paul, Ray, Nelson

Helen and Dotty

Howard, Ray, Helen, Dorothy, Mil, Jimmy, Ray Malan.

Ray, civilian

Ray and Helen

Ray, Helen, Ed, Mil, June, Mary

Helen

Helen and Ray

Lee

I asked James Singley to tell the story of the "Hotel" in Japan, and he very kindly told me the story.

James Singley volunteered to stay in Japan after he had enough points to come home. The following is an account of his experiences starting in Okinawa:

When we were on Okinawa and advancing to take Naha and the hills above Naha, one of the many caves in the hills had a steel door. When we blew the door off, the cave was full of stamps and Jap money. I got several sheets of different stamps (I still have them). Someone got a sea bag off one of the tanks with us, and we filled it with the money and sent it to the rear to be put on one of our supply trucks, and promptly forgot all about it.

After we were in Japan and the 4th Marines were turned into an MP company, some of us were stationed at the downtown Yokosuka police station. We were still feeling bitter toward the Japs. We had an interpreter who claimed he was an American Jap and had a bank account in a Frisco bank, and was in Japan visiting when the war broke out. He hated the Japs.

The 4th Marines as MPs stood guard duty all around Yokosuka and at the Navy pier. We had orders to confiscate all cartons of cigarettes from all personnel entering Yokosuka, to control black market. Cigarettes were selling at $20 per carton and cost us $2 per carton. All cigarettes from outlying posts were turned in to downtown police headquarters each evening; then we were to turn them in to the MP headquarters at the base.

Our interpreter told us he could sell the cigarettes for $20 a carton (Jap money), and we decided that was a good idea to sell them and get all that Jap money. We would raid the place the cigarettes were sold and get back the cigarettes and keep the money; then turn the cigarettes into headquarters. It turned out to be a real good idea, and we enjoyed it so much we sometimes sold the cigarettes two or three times a night before we turned them in to MP headquarters. This shows some of our contempt for the Japs, as we thought this was a lot of fun.

One night when we had handfuls of Jap money, somebody said, "The money looks just like that money from the cave in Okinawa," and we all agreed. The next morning we went down to the motor pool and asked our buddy if the sea bag was still on one of his trucks. He said, "I think it is," and it was, and all that money was just like the money we had been getting from our cigarette sales. We had more Jap money than we knew what to do with.

The mayor and the police chief of Yokosuka were having a party for us two or three times a week in the first floor facilities of a three-story gray glazed tile hotel in downtown Yokosuka. We discussed what to do with the money at the many parties. Finally the interpreter said, "Why don't you buy this hotel building?" So we did. He made all the arrangements about the deed and all papers.

The ground floor of the hotel had a nice jewelry store, a barber shop, meeting room and some other business and covered a quarter of a block.

The top two stories were crowded with refugees from bombed-out Yokohama and Tokyo.

We decided we wanted the top two stories for our parties, so we told everyone to be out at 4 o'clock one day. The mayor and chief of police were to enforce this. At 4 o'clock that day we went with the chief of police to each room and threw anybody and everything out the window that we didn't want.

There were 12 of us in on the deal for the hotel, and we had one continuous party there the rest of our time in Yokosuka.

When we were ready to leave Japan, Captain Codispoti had "acquired" a truck load of priceless antique Japanese souvenirs. He asked us to get him a covered recon so he could bring it all back to the States. We Marines had no recons with canvas tops, so we swiped two army recons and leaded in the star and repainted them Marine colors. (We swiped two because we thought if Captain Codispoti could take a truck load of souvenirs aboard ship, we could take a truck load of beer.) Seventy cases lasted almost halfway to San Diego. Aboard ship we would get cases of beer every night and drink it on the fan tail of the ship.

We got caught a few times by the O.D. (Officer of the Day), and he always kicked our beer over the side and reported us to Captain Codispoti (Ha). Nothing ever happened.

One night we thought about our hotel in Japan. We had the deed and papers with us. One of the 12 said he was going back to Japan after he was discharged. (I forgot his name), so we all signed our hotel over to him. If he went back to Japan and ran the hotel, he would sure be a millionaire today.

Joe Bibby married Mary Ann when he came back to the States for the Marine Air Corps.

Robert Lindsay was divorced after the war. He met and married a lovely girl named Gini.

2nd Marine Raider Bn. Co. H on Bougainville from Squad 3

James Singley — James' father and Marguerite's mother grew up in the same neighborhood, south of Green City, Missouri. The families lived in Green City and were neighbors, so James and Marguerite always knew each other. It was not until after WWII that they became an "item." A blind date hadn't worked out very well, and the following Saturday Marguerite was selling poppies for the American Legion Auxiliary and approached James to buy a poppy — well, two — one for his date. Later that evening he called and asked her to wear the date's poppy. That was about May 30, 1946. They became engaged August 26, 1946, and were married June 7, 1947 at the Green City Methodist Church.

They have four children: Susan Poland, born 4-24-53; Cynthia, born 5-12-55; Dennis, born 9-10-56, and David, born 10-8-64. A son-in-law, Dan; daughter-in-laws Julie and Lew Ellen. A grandson, Preston Poland, born 4-25-85. Grandaughter Taryn Poland born 10-30-87.

Marguerite says: "We still have the poppy, and our friends, Ray and Helen, gave us a 'Precious Moments' Marine, and we have it and a 'Precious Moments' poppy girl in a special place."

The five remaining members of 10-man Squad 2

Rusty Tratebas was discharged from the Corps in January 1946 and tried college life for a year at Valparaiso University. His stepfather passed away the next summer and left two young boys and his mom to take care of — so Rusty started farming the family farm and working on construction. This kept him busy (and broke), so he managed to stay a "happy" bachelor until the spring of '54, when a friend of his talked him into a blind date with a girl who worked with his wife at the local hospital. They went roller skating on that first date, and per Rusty, "I fell in more than one way."

Edith was an R.N. and had been raised on a farm about 30 miles south of Terre Haute, Indiana. They went together two years and were married on June 23, 1956, in Valparaiso, Indiana.

Edith became ill in January 1963 and passed away on May 24, 1963, when their daughter, Kathy, was nine months old. Edith's father had passed away just seven weeks before, so Rusty moved son David and daughter Kathy into Grandma Jo's home, and she helped him raise a couple of good kids.

Kathy has left the nest and has her Masters Degree and a good job with Delta Faucet in Indy. Dave has stayed at home and works as a machinist at a local bearing factory and farms in his "spare time."

Rusty says Grandma Jo is the greatest mother-in-law a fellow could ask for! Dave says the cooking is the best and plans on staying.

Norman Korsmeyer — Betty says: I was acquainted with Norm and his family as his sister, Dorothy, is married to my brother Lafe. I remembered seeing Norm at the farm when he was home on leave. I was still in high school, but I thought at the time he was pretty neat. And I still do.

I left the community in September 1947 to attend nursing school. So it wasn't until the fall of 1951 that we really met.

We had our first date the last weekend in September, became engaged the last weekend in October, and were married the second weekend in December 1951. We moved to the family farm where our two daughters and two sons were born.

Farming has been good to us, and we are thankful for all our blessings.

Raymond Strohmeyer — Ray met Wanda a few days after he came home from the Marines, in November 1945. She was 17 and he was 22. Ray's sister was married to Wanda's brother after Ray had joined the Marines. He didn't know about Wanda until after the war. They told him she was red-headed and had a real temper. She was working in a cafe when four men came in and one of them pinched her. She picked up a beer bottle and whacked him on the head and knocked him out cold.

Ray says he had gone to help his dad and was waiting for him by the door when a real pretty red-headed girl came in, and Papa turned around and said, "This is Wanda." Papa liked her so that was good enough for me. I think — with me — that it was love at first sight. The strange thing was that I could talk to her. I was scared to death of women, and around girls I was plumb tongue-tied, but around her, I wasn't bashful. We could talk up a storm.

I just got to see her a couple more times before she moved to Bowie, Texas, with her mother, brother and sister, and she began to date a guy there and had become engaged.

In June, Ray went with his sister's husband to visit Wanda's family. He says: "We all had a good time that weekend. I started to go out past her, and she looked up at me with such a lost and questioning look in her eyes, I couldn't resist leaning down and kissing her, and I whispered, 'I love you.' "

She had a date that night. She was gone about 15 minutes. She had told her date she couldn't go out because she had company. She told Ray much later that little kiss was the sweetest she ever got, and the reason she broke her date that night — and later her engagement.

Wanda moved back to stay with her sister and started to work in a cafe closer to where Ray worked. Ray would walk her home from work every night. In September he took her to a dance. He said, "Honey, when are we going to get married?" On Saturday morning two weeks later they went to the courthouse and got married by the justice of the peace.

For the next 48 years, 9 months and 20 days, she was the best helpmate a man could ever have. She died of cancer on July 11, 1995.

Bill Carroll was a friend of Joe Mangel who was in the 3rd Raiders, but they didn't meet until they were in Weapons Company together on Guadalcanal. They went to Guam and Okinawa together. After the war Bill was working a summer job in Ohio near Cleveland, so went to visit Joe, who had a sister named Annie.

That is how Bill and Annie met. They were married November 28, 1946, during Bill's Thanksgiving Day break from college. They have one daughter and three sons.

Bill and Annie's 50th anniversary will be on Thanksgiving Day this year (1996).

Ray Merrell — Helen and I were engaged December 19, 1945, six days after I arrived home. We were married Easter Sunday, April 21, 1946, at the Christian Union Church, near Sweet Springs, Missouri.

We have two wonderful children: Deborah Sue, born October 22, 1953, and Robert Alan, born April 13, 1955. A son-in-law, Jim Hopper, and daughter-in-law, Deborah Lynn, and three grandchildren: Jason Charles Ireland, born December 9, 1976; Richard Alan Merrell, born September 13, 1980; Lynn Marie Merrell, born May 29, 1982, and a step-grandson, Chris Hopper, born September 6, 1970. They "all" had a great celebration for us on our 50th anniversary in 1996.

Ray (Tex) Strohmeyer, Ray Merrell, Bill Carroll, Norm Korsmeyer, Rusty Tratebas. Five remaining members of Squad 2, 1996.

2nd Marine Raider Bn. Co. H, Squad 2
Our 10-Man Squad on Bougainville

THOR THOSTENSON — Squad Leader
Guadalcanal, Bougainville, KIA on Iwo Jima

NORMAN KORSMEYER — Fire Squad Leader
Guadalcanal, Bougainville, wounded on Iwo Jima.

RUSTY TRATEBAS
Guadalcanal (wounded), Bougainville (wounded),
Iwo Jima (wounded)

STUART CAMPBELL (RAINBOW)
Guadalcanal (Silver Star), KIA on Bougainville

TEX STROHMEYER
Bougainville, Emirau, Guam, Okinawa (wounded),
Occupation of Japan

BILL CARROLL
Bougainville, Emirau, Guam (wounded),
Okinawa (wounded), Occupation of Japan

KENNETH FRANTZ
Guadalcanal, Bougainville, Deceased

RICHIE SPATH
Guadalcanal, Bougainville, Iwo Jima (wounded),
Deceased

R.D. McDOWELL
Guadalcanal, Bougainville, Deceased

RAY MERRELL
Bougainville, Emirau, Guam, Okinawa, Occupation of Japan

—

From Squad 3
JAMES SINGLEY
Bougainville, Emirau, Guam, Okinawa, Occupation of Japan

From Co. G
ROBERT LINDSAY
Bougainville, Emirau, Guam, Okinawa (wounded),
Deceased

2nd Marine Raider Bn. Co. H

10 men to a squad .... Thor Thostenson, Squad Leader
30 men to a platoon .... Lt. Skip Daly, Platoon Leader
250 men to a company .... Capt. Robert Burnett
1000 men to a battalion .... Col. Alan Shapley
(plus weapons platoon, machine gun and mortars)

We made very close ties to our buddies in the Marine Corps, by drilling, training, working, digging foxholes, being shot at, buddies being wounded or killed. And by sharing our hopes and dreams.

Left to right: James Singley, Ray Strohmeyer, Norm Korsmeyer,
Bill Carroll, Ray Merrell, Rusty Tratebas.
Members of 2nd Marine Raider Bn. Co. H
on New Caledonia, Bougainville and Guadalcanal

Five remaining members of 10-man Squad 2
and James Singley of Squad 3

Picture taken at Norm Korsmeyer's home
near Beardstown, Illinois, September 2000

- I enlisted in the Marines 11-17-42.
- My brother Nelson (Ned) was inducted in the Navy 12-31-43.
- My brother Paul was inducted in the Navy 8-14-44.

DATES SPENT ON SHIPS — WORLD WAR II

San Diego, California to Noumea, New Caledonia — U.S.S. Mt. Vernon, March 11-26, 1943

Noumea, New Caledonia to Guadalcanal — U.S.S. President Hayes, October 4-11, 1943

Guadalcanal to Efate — U.S.S. George Clymer, October 13-15, 1943

Efate to Espirtu Santo — U.S.S. George Clymer, October 15-23, 1943

Espiritu Santo to Guadalcanal — U.S.S. George Clymer, October 25-27, 1943

Guadalcanal to Bougainville — U.S.S. George Clymer, October 28, 1943 to November 1, 1943

Bougainville to Guadalcanal — U.S.S. President Hayes, January 12-14, 1944

Maneuvers — U.S.S. Warren, March 8-10, 1944

Guadalcanal to Emirau — U.S.S. Callaway, March 17-20, 1944

Emirau to Guadalcanal — U.S.S. DuPage, April 12-15, 1944

Maneuvers — U.S.S. Ormsby, May 12-14, 1944

Guadalcanal to Guam — U.S.S. Ormsby, June 4-July 21, 1944

Guam to Guadalcanal — U.S. ATS Pennat — August 28-September 8, 1944

Maneuvers — U.S.S. McIntyre, Off Guadalcanal

Guadalcanal to Okinawa — U.S.S. McIntyre, March 12-April 1, 1945

Okinawa to Guam — LST 1110, July 6-16, 1945

Guam to Japan — U.S.S. Grimes, August 15-30, 1945

Japan to USA — U.S.S. Calvert, November 3-22, 1945.

My Many Addresses

November '42
Pvt. Louis R. Merrell
Platoon 1127
Recruit Depot, Marine Corps Base
San Diego, California

January '43
Infantry School Co. D.
11th Replacement Battalion
Fleet Marine Force Training
Center
Camp Elliott
San Diego, California

March '43
11th Replacement Battalion Fleet
Postmaster
San Francisco, California

May '43
2nd Marine Raiders Battalion
Fleet Postmaster
San Francisco, California

June '43
Co. H. 2nd Marine Raider Bn.
Fleet Post Office
San Francisco, California

**The following are all to
Fleet Post Office,
San Francisco, California**

September '43
PFC Louis R. Merrell
Co. H 2nd Marine Raider Bn.
2nd Marine Regiment Provisional
(PFC August '43)

February '44
Regimental Weapons Co.
4th Marines
1st Mac — FMF

April '44
Regimental Weapons Co.
Reinforced
4th Marines III Amp. Corps

Regimental Weapons Co.
4th Marines Reinforced
1st Provisional Marine Brigade

September '44
Regimental Weapons Co.
4th Marines Reinforced
6th Marine Division

November '44
Regimental Weapons Co.
4th Marines Reinforced

Cpl. Regimental Weapons Co.
4th Marines
(Cpl. Dec.) 12-4-44 USMC
(Sgt. Dec.) 12-21-44 USMCV

Sgt. L.R. Merrell U.S.M.C.
Regimental Weapons Co.
4th Marines
6th Marine Division

June '45
S/Sgt. Louis R. Merrell
Regimental Weapons Co.
4th Marines
6th Marine Division

131

Tuesday, February 20, 1996

Raiders from 2nd Bn. H Co. were introduced to the Arizona Senate by Bob Chastain 2H. He said, "There are Marine Raiders in the Gallery, but don't worry, they turned in their submachine guns, automatic rifles, machetes and hand grenades when they left the Marines over 50 years ago.

"Marine Raiders were the elite troops of the Marine Corps in WWII. They landed in rubber boots from submarines and destroyers on hit-and-run campaigns. They did long combat and reconnaissance patrols behind enemy lines. They were always first to land on beaches with the toughest enemy resistance.

"To be a Raider, you volunteered twice: once for the Marines and once for the Raiders. After that you learned your lesson.

"Visiting us today from H. Co., 2nd Raider Battalion are:

Ray Strohmeyer — Joshua, Texas

Ray and Helen Merrell — Liberty, Missouri

Bill and Annie Carroll — Florence, Oregon

Russell Tratebas — Kouts, Indiana

Norm and Betty Korsmeyer — Beardstown, Illinois

James and Marguerite Singley — Green City, Missouri and
Florence, Arizona

"The executive officer of the 2nd Battalion was James Roosevelt, son of the Democrat President of the U.S. at that time. They thought since he was the President's son that they would maybe not get too many tough assignments. After the Battle of Midway and Makin Island, James transferred out, and they went on to fight on the isles of the Pacific on Guadalcanal, Bougainville, Emirau, Guam, Iwo Jima, Okinawa and the occupation of Japan.

"They waded many streams, rivers, swamps, and cut many trails through the jungle. They swatted thousands of mosquitos, ate cold rations and dug hundreds of foxholes. They also dodged a lot of shrapnel and bullets and managed to collect a total of seven Purple Hearts.

"Their wives are the real heroes. They married them, reintroduced them into society and got them recivilized.

"Members, these men, you could trust them with your life. I know because I served in H Co. with them."

Marine Drive built by the Seabees. Taken January 1944 as we were leaving Bougainville.

Gung Ho!   Semper Fi!

Editor's Note: *Mr. Paul Donelly (in USA Today) wrote "America's WWII generation saved the world because it had to be done, and no one else was available to do it."*

I am proud to say my husband was one of them.

— Helen

*First wave —
Guam invasion.
Garcia, Rawlings,
Drumm, Palmer,
Goeble.*

*Marines on
the beach,
Guam
invasion,
7-21-44.*

*Left to right: Morley, Bartley, Spencer, Nolen, Reed,
Singley. Front row: DePung, Flynn, Russell, Slobodzian.
After the Piva Trail battle on Bougainville.*

Russell and Goebels on Guadalcanal

Merrell, Tratebas, Korsmeyer, on Efate Island, cooking our own meals.

Joe Harrison, Rusty Tratebas, Ray Merrell, Ted Czeski. Marine Raider Reunion, Scottsdale, Arizona, 1991.

Back row: Rusty Tratebas, Norm Korsmeyer, James Singley, Bill Carroll, Skip Daly. Front row: Betty Korsmeyer, Marguerite Singley, Ray Merrell, Helen Merrell, Annie Carroll. Washington, D.C. '92 Reunion.

Joe Bibby, Mary Anne Bibby, Hilaire Daly, Skip Daly.
Minneapolis Marine Reunion, 1993.

Back row: Geo. Finley, Rusty Tratebas, Ray Merrell, Norm Korsmeyer, James Singley, Bill Carroll, Joe Harrison. Front row: Betty Korsmeyer, Marguerite Singley, Annie Carroll, Eleanor Harrison. Las Vegas Reunion, 1994

Al Kaminsky, Rusty Tratebas. Las Vegas Reunion, 1994.

136

Betty Korsmeyer raising her flags on Mt. Suribachi (landing beach in background). 50th Anniversary of Iwo Jima, February 1995.

Left to right: Norm Korsmeyer, Ray (Tex) Strohmeyer, Ray Merrell, Rusty Tratebas, James Singley, Bob Seaman, Bill Carroll. At Norm and Betty Korsmeyer's home, July 1999.

Bob and Phosia Chastain, Hilaire Daly. Marine Raider Reunion, Chicago, Illinois, 2000.

Ray looking at a BAR at Marine Raider Museum in Richmond, Virginia.

Doors that post the names of all Marine Raiders at Museum, Richmond, Virginia, 1992.

Skip Daly and Ray Merrell, Marine Raider Reunion, Minneapolis, Minnesota, 1993.

Ray and Joe Bibby at Museum.

Betty Korsmeyer, Bill Carroll, Annie Carroll, Marguerite Singley, Helen Merrell, James Singley, Rusty Tratebas, Norm Korsmeyer (standing), Ray Merrell, Branson, Missouri, September 1998.

Helen and Ray Merrell at 6th Marine Division Reunion Picnic, Arlington, Texas, April 1999.

What a nice surprise to get your memories of the Marine Corps. I started reading it and couldn't put it down. I'm on page 24. There were things you did that made me laugh, and also made me cry. I'm so glad you kept your wonderful sense of humor. That helped to pull you through. I'm so glad you had wonderful in-law parents. I was lucky that way, too. You didn't have time at home to sit under shade trees. There was always work to do or something more important. Thanks again for your thoughtfulness.

> *Ernie Wheeler*
> *St. Louis, Missouri*

Received pamphlet on Marine Corps History. Have read it over and really enjoyed it.

> *Nelson Merrell*
> *Palm Harbor, Florida*

Thanks for the book. I have already read it. I'm now passing it around for my family to read. Nick is reading it now. Helen, you did a great job. So interesting.

> *Mil and Raymond Malan*
> *Marshall, Missouri*

Thank you so much for your Marine history booklet! I've read every bit and Les is on it, it's simply a treasure, but frightening, brought back all the depressing time of waiting for all our Marines, Sailors and Soldiers to come home.

> *Leola and Les Wheeler*
> *Brooksville, Florida*

Thanks so much for the book. I have really enjoyed each page. Helen, you did a magnificent job putting it all together. I read it clear thru the first night and reviewed it since. Some pages I cried and others I laughed at some of Ray's cute remarks. What a wonderful book for Debbie and Alan and family .

> *Leola Gilmore*
> *Prairie Village, Kansas*

Gary read Ray's book and was so intrigued.

> *Leola Gilmore*

"The Three Little Sisters," I remember the song. The picture of the three of you brought back so many memories. I had some outfits just like the three of you.

Annie Carroll

Sounds like a "love story" to me.

Ernie Wheeler

We've both finished THE book. Bill says it's the most honest and modest portrayal of a part of a person's life that he's ever read, and a labor of love on Helen's part. We're truly impressed. Bless you both.

Bill and Annie Carroll
Florence, Oregon

Dad, Jim Lenge at Golden Oaks just called to tell you how much he appreciated getting a copy of your book. He has read it cover to cover, and is going to read it again. He said it is one of the most touching, informative and charming books he has ever read. He said it is a beautiful book.

Debbie

Really enjoyed your book. Brought tears to my eyes on many occasions. You guys are something else.

Norm and Betty Korsmeyer
Beardstown, Illinois

I sure did appreciate you sending me a copy of the book you wrote. It was real good. Maybe your book will inspire me to write.

Ever your Buddy,
Raymond Strohmeyer
Joshua, Texas

Gung Ho!